BRAVO Principal!

Building Relationships with Actions That Value Others

Sandra Harris

EYE ON EDUCATION
6 DEPOT WAY WEST, SUITE 106
LARCHMONT, NY 10538
(914) 833–0551
(914) 833–0761 fax
www.eyeoneducation.com

Library of Congress Cataloging-in-Publication Data

Harris, Sandra, 1946-
    Bravo principal! : building relationships with actions that value others / by Sandra Harris.
        p. cm.
    ISBN 1-930556-78-0
    1. School principals--Professional relationships 2. Educational leadership. I. Title.

LB2831.9 H37 2004
371.2'012--dc22

2004043218

10 9 8 7 6 5 4 3 2 1

Editorial and production services provided by
Richard H. Adin Freelance Editorial Services
52 Oakwood Blvd., Poughkeepsie, NY 12603-4112
(914-471-3566)

Also Available from EYE ON EDUCATION

What Great Principals Do *Differently*:
15 Things That Matter Most
Todd Whitaker

Dealing with Difficult Teachers, Second Edition
Todd Whitaker

Dealing with Difficult Parents
(And with Parents in Difficult Situations)
Todd Whitaker and Douglas Fiore

Motivating & Inspiring Teachers:
The Educational Leader's Guide for Building Staff Morale
Todd Whitaker, Beth Whitaker, and Dale Lumpa

What Great Teachers Do *Differently*:
14 Things That Matter Most
Todd Whitaker

Supervision Across the Content Areas
Sally J. Zepeda and R. Stewart Mayers

The Principal as Instructional Leader:
A Handbook for Supervisors
Sally J. Zepeda

Instructional Leadership for School Improvement
Sally J. Zepeda

Standards of Practice for Teachers A Brief Handbook
P. Diane Frey, Mary Jane Smart, and Sue A. Walker

Achievement Now!
How To Assure No Child is Left Behind
Dr. Donald J. Fielder

The ISLLC Standards in Action:
A Principal's Handbook
Carol Engler

Harnessing the Power of Resistance:
A Guide for Educators
Jared Scherz

Teaching Matters:
Motivating & Inspiring Yourself
Todd and Beth Whitaker

101 Answers for New Teachers and Their Mentors:
Effective Teaching Tips for Daily Classroom Use
Annette L. Breaux

Data Analysis for Continuous School Improvement
Victoria L. Bernhardt

School Leader Internship: Developing, Monitoring,
and Evaluating Your Leadership Experience
Gary Martin, William Wright, and Arnold Danzig

Handbook on Teacher Evaluation:
Assessing and Improving Performance
James Stronge & Pamela Tucker

Handbook on Educational Specialist Evaluation:
Assessing & Improving Performance
James Stronge & Pamela Tucker

Handbook on Teacher Portfolios
for Evaluation and Professional Development
Pamela Tucker & James Stronge

The Confrontational Parent:
A Practical Guide for School Leaders
Dr. Charles M. Jaksec III

Beyond Measure:
Neglected Elements of Accountability in Schools
Edited by Patricia E. Holland

Table of Contents

Introduction

A Hand on the Wall

There is nothing unusual about a hot day in August in Arizona. But this day seemed unusually hot. Still, my husband and I decided to explore the red rocks around Sedona. We left the highway and followed a bumpy dirt road for miles and miles. Finally, we saw what we were looking for: a small, unobtrusive sign that read, Indian Cliff Dwellings. We parked the car and climbed out into the hot Arizona sun. After a 15-minute walk up a winding path, we stood in front of an ancient cliff dwelling built into the massive red rocks.

The park ranger shared stories of what life had been like for the ancient people who had lived in these cliff dwellings anywhere from 1,000 to 3,000 years ago. In some places the walls were dark, remnants of the smoke that had spiraled upward seeking an exit. Other parts of the cliff walls were filled with pictographs that included ladders reaching to the sun, stick figures, and wildlife.

As the ranger was telling us that the darkest red pictographs were nearly 3,000 years old, my eyes fell on the outline of a tiny red hand about two feet from the ground on the wall. I heard the ranger say, " ...and over here, we have the outline of a hand, probably of a four- or five-year-old child." In my mind, I could see a small Indian child watching as the father drew stories on the wall. I could see the father, holding the leftover red-clay paint in his hand, motion to the child to come nearer. The child walked eagerly to the father, and spreading his fingers open wide, placed a small hand in the paint. Then, carefully, the child began to consider the rock, looking for an open, flat space. In my mind, I could imagine the father bending over to carefully guide the tiny wrist, as the small hand pressed onto the rock face. Now, 3000 years later, the action of a father and a small child remained, a visible imprint and a living testimony of a people who had lived among these cliffs.

Today, in the twenty-first century, we are busy, busy people. Rarely do we realize the tremendous impact that our singular actions have on the world, until we come face to face with something like a small red hand, still imprinted upon the face of an ancient rock. Yet, 3,000 years later that small red hand called out and reminded me of the importance and the often long-lasting effect of our actions.

This book is for leaders, specifically, school principals; although, the more I think about it, the more I believe that the actions discussed here can benefit leaders in any situation. After 35 years in education, I still read the books and the studies that share information about how to build effective schools. I know that effective schools emphasize academics, high standards, good teaching, and continued learning for everyone on the school campus. Yet, one common theme is central to all of these studies: the importance of strong leadership that values teachers, students, and the wider community. The single most important person in bringing about effective leadership to the school is the principal. In other words, it is most often through principal-leadership actions that schools become effective or through lack of principal-leadership actions that schools become ineffective.

Even though the principal is clearly the identified leader of the school, the strength of the relationship between a leader and the individuals who are led is often unclear. At the same time, no principal can be the only leader in the school and still be effective. We all know of schools where there are strong teacher leaders, student leaders, and community leaders who partner together with a shared vision to build effective schools. Linda Lambert argues that leadership is reciprocal and this act of "reciprocity helps us build relationships of mutual regard" (2003, p. 2) within the community that emphasize shared purpose, caring, integrity, and truthfulness.

How can principals build the kind of reciprocal leadership relationships with teachers, students, and the community that will strengthen schools? The key lies in building relationships that value all stakeholders: faculty, staff, students, parents, and community members. I call it BRAVO—Building Relationships with Actions that Value Others. These actions fall into six categories:

1. Actions that are Empowering
2. Actions that are Supportive
3. Actions that are Respectful
4. Actions that Challenge the Imagination
5. Actions that Uphold High Standards
6. Actions that are Courageous

The following six chapters discuss each of these important values and describe how BRAVO principals ACT on these values to build relationships among teachers, students, and others that establish a climate for effective schools to thrive.

It is never enough to dream of good ideas or talk about doing good things, it is only when we put the paint on our hand and carefully press it into the face of the wall that the act can be seen. As school leaders, it is only when our *actions* value others that we leave an impression that can effectively change our schools into places that value others.

1

Actions that Are Empowering: Give Power Away

"Leaders accept and act on the paradox of power: *We become most powerful when we give our own power away.*"

(Kouzes & Posner, 2002, p. 285)

More years ago than I care to say, I taught in a small rural school. There was no teacher's lounge, so when my class was at PE or music, I often sat at a desk in the hall planning lessons or grading papers. Nearly everyday the kindergarten class passed this desk on its way outside for recess. Each time the children passed by, a little boy in the class would look at me, smile, and say, "You sure are pretty." Of course, I always gave him a delighted smile before I returned to my work. This happened so often that I told my husband and friends about it, laughing, of course, but, still flattered. After all, a compliment is a compliment, even if it comes from a five year old!

One day as I sat at the desk grading papers, once again the kindergarten class walked by. Sure enough, my little admirer smiled and said, "You sure are pretty." I acknowledged his compliment with a smile and turned back to my papers. Then I heard him say to the little fellow in front of him, "I say that every day. Doesn't matter who's sitting there."

To my chagrin, this little kindergartner was giving lip service to something that he did not really believe. In today's atmosphere of participative, shared decision making, many principals do the same thing. They often say they believe in "empowering teachers," and many even organize site-based committees. In fact, in some states, such as Texas for example, site-based committees are actually mandated. Yet, it is not unusual for teachers, parents, and even students to tell me that they "sit on the committees" but often their input is only minimally considered, if at all. Just like the little kindergartner who said what he did not really believe, too often, principals give lip service to the idea of empowering others, but their actions clearly indicate that this has little value. To many principals, the notion of sharing power is considered a weakening of their strength as a school leader.

Empower Others Through Creating a Shared Vision

Since the late 1980s and early 1990s, educational leaders, such as Andy Hargreaves (1994) and Thomas Sergiovanni (1992), have emphasized the importance of empowering teachers by giving them opportunities to make decisions that facilitate a positive school climate. The importance of empowerment was further emphasized in a study I conducted a few years ago. I asked 123 teachers what their principals did to promote a positive school climate that supported teacher quality and student learning (Harris, 2000). All the teachers indicated the importance of being empowered, and one out of four teachers said the single most important act their principal did was to empower them to share in identifying and clarifying the school vision. The teachers went on to comment that this was important because it demonstrated the principal's trust in them professionally and in their potential as leaders.

Restore the Vision

Often, the very act of being involved in making school decisions enhances feelings of responsibility to student learning, not just because it is what teachers are supposed to do, but because it renews their vision of why they became teachers in the first place: to help young people. Recently, a student in one of my principal preparation classes told me that after teaching for ten years, she had considered leaving teaching. She no longer enjoyed teaching, did not feel that she was doing anything worthwhile, and, ultimately, felt powerless as an educator. She was so busy with lesson plans, grading papers, and testing, she could not even remember why she had become a teacher.

This teacher's school faculty rotated every year onto a very inactive, very uninvolved site-based council, and it had become her turn to serve. This year the school had a new principal. In August, she had gone to the new principal, explained her "burnout" and tried to get out of serving on the committee. He told her he did not want to force her to be on the committee, but he did want her to at least begin the year by serving on it. "I served all year. When the year was up," she told me, "I had seen a whole new aspect of the processes that impacted student learning. The principal began the year by engaging the committee in discussing *our* vision for the school. He listened to *our* suggestions and many of them were actually implemented. For the first time in a long time, I remembered the enthusiasm with which I began my first year of teaching and, to my shock, I began to feel that same excitement again." Now, two years later, this teacher is not only still teaching, but is enrolled in a program to earn her master's degree in the principalship.

Frame the Vision
Around Student Success

Sergiovanni points out that through purposing, school leaders "restore meaning to what schools do" (p. 72). In the action of empowerment the purposeful vision to improve schools for all children becomes a shared vision between principals, teachers, students, and others. This collaborative framing of the school vision emphasizes the connection between what we are doing and how it contributes to student success. Principals who build relationships with actions that value others empower others by involving them in creating this shared vision of student success.

One of the teachers in my study commented that as her principal involved the faculty in creating the school vision, he continuously reminded them that student success had to be at the very heart of that vision. For example, as the faculty reviewed the academic indicator test data, it was noted that math scores had decreased steadily over the past three years. The decline was small, but there was a decline. The site-based committee responsible for creating the campus plan committed the next several meetings to considering this problem. Committee members discussed texts being used, budget monies available, teacher experience, changing community demographics, and much more. But always, she noted, the principal began each discussion by asking what decisions should be made to help students be successful. When decisions were being reached, he would ask again, "Now, how will this contribute to student success?" In other words, the principal constantly kept the vision for student success at the forefront of all decisions. Teachers involved in this process agreed that this contributed to their sense of empowerment to help all students achieve.

Empower Others Through Establishing Trust

Empowerment does not happen in a vacuum. It can only occur in an atmosphere where mutual trust is established. Principals must be willing to trust the wisdom and abilities of teachers, students, and community leaders. They show trust in community leaders when they invite them onto the school campus to participate in planning and enriching school activities. Principals actively show trust in students when they listen and act on their input regarding school issues. Principals show trust in teachers when they involve them in educational decisions, treat them professionally, and give them the freedom to teach. They also establish trust with teachers through delegating responsibly.

Give Teachers the Freedom to Teach

In my survey, one teacher said, "[My principal] trusts our judgment by letting us teach. He doesn't hover over us." Another pointed out that "My principal is a gentleman of action but few words. He will basically leave you alone in the classroom as long as teaching results are good." Another said, "He gives teachers the power to move forward. He... has given us the 'go' to do what it takes to get the job done. In other words, do what you know works..." (Harris, 2000, p. 37).

One challenge of principals is, of course, that of motivating their staffs. Certainly there are ways to motivate, such as incentive pay, career ladder steps, allowing teachers to leave early on a birthday, and others, but my experience has been that, whereas these are nice, the best way to motivate faculty involves making the job of teaching itself be rewarding. Mihalyi Csikszentmihalyi (1990) calls this "flow"; people experience this when they are so involved in an activity that it results in a high level of personal satisfaction and enhances feelings of competence. Principals who trust teachers help them experience flow by giving them the freedom to teach and to make decisions within their own classrooms.

Trust is the foundation for empowerment, for when principals trust others they are liberated to share their power by giving power away. They know that giving power away strengthens, rather than weakens, their leadership role. Giving their power away motivates others to contribute and to work harder. I know very little about flowers, but a few years ago, my next door neighbor planted a lily in my front yard. I haven't done anything to that plant, except water it; yet, this summer there were a dozen lilies in my little flower garden. Power is like that lily. As it is given away to empower others and nourished with trust, it enhances rather than diminishes.

Delegate Responsibly

Delegation of responsibilities is an excellent way for principals to act on their trust of faculty, students, and others. I remember my first year as a principal. The job was overwhelming. At a faculty meeting, I delegated certain responsibilities regarding playground duty to various teachers. I knew that if I checked on them constantly, I might as well have kept the responsibility myself, and no one would feel empowered. But I also knew that I could not expect, what I was not willing to inspect. Therefore, even though I trusted that the teachers would handle this responsibility properly, together we agreed on an appropriate follow-up that included me. Later, one of the teachers told me that she respected this. Before, when jobs had been delegated to teachers, they felt as though the principal was just trying to "pass off" responsibilities that he did not want to have. By being involved in the follow-up, teachers felt as though we were part of a team working together to see that playground duty went smoothly. In fact, sharing the responsibility actually increased our trust in one another, which made it easier to share power in the future.

Empower Others Through Building Leadership at Every Level

Power is certainly important. After all, it is through power that we influence others and accomplish important goals. An important component of power is activated when we use *our power* to empower others. In other words, power is most effective when it is not power *over* but power *to* and power *with*. It is in the action of sharing power that we empower others.

Linda Lambert provides us with another challenge to empower others when she reminds us that "everyone has the right, responsibility, and capability to be a leader" (2003, p. 4).

Teachers feel that being empowered demonstrates their value to themselves, as well as to others. And when they are not empowered, they feel devalued, weak, and, as one of my students said, "unable to make good things happen for kids at school."

Share Power with Teachers

I once taught for a principal who had led this particular school for nearly 15 years. The school appeared well-run and the students were well-behaved. Everyone considered it the place to teach. The first month I was there, I loved it. The second month I was not so sure. Everything that teachers did had to be approved by the principal! If I had a question and went to the lead teacher for help, she would listen, nod her head, and say, "Well, we'll have to ask the principal about that."

In November, I was assigned to head up the annual Christmas program. I was delighted and called a meeting of my committee to discuss ideas. One teacher who had been at the school for several years was appointed to take notes. As the committee began sharing ideas, I noticed that she wrote nothing. Finally, I said, "Why aren't you taking notes? We won't remember any of this!" She responded, "What difference does it make about our ideas? Do you really think Mr. Smith will let us do any of this? This is HIS school and HIS Christmas program!" Later that week, I met with Mr. Smith and shared our ideas. She was right. He listened politely, thanked me for heading the committee, and even told me how much he appreciated our work. Then, he promptly told me how the program would be done!

When I was assigned to lead the Christmas program committee, I went to the teacher next door and shared how nervous I was about this assignment because I wanted to do a really good job. She laughed and said, "Don't worry, it will be the easiest committee you have ever led." Now, I understand why she had said that.

Today, as I reflect on Mr. Smith and his leadership, I am not sure if he was a victim of a leadership style that failed to acknowledge the importance of empowering others, if he did not trust teachers, or if he was just a power-monger! I do know that as a principal, he made me feel unimportant and unnecessary. I was glad to leave that school.

Another principal I knew voiced all of the right things. She talked about how much she cared for *her* faculty. She put notes in their boxes thanking them for various jobs she considered well done. She read lesson plans and put little smiley faces on them. But, one day, ten of her staff of 18 teachers went to their superintendent and threatened to not return the next year because they felt like "puppets on a string... she does not trust us to make any professional decisions on our own." Sadly, I think this principal really did care for her staff. But she viewed power in one way only—how *she* could accomplish *her* vision at the school. She simply did not realize that her need to control faculty resulted in a faculty powerless to lead.

Principals who share power with teachers talk about "our" school, but more than that, they build relationships with teachers that foster and nurture strong leadership skills. They use their power to implement the good ideas that others have. Then, at every opportunity, they acknowledge faculty, students, parents, and others publicly and privately for their good ideas and their hard work. Empowering principals share the accolades; they never miss an opportunity to sing the praises of others; and they actively seek ways to shine the spotlight on those who work quietly and well behind the scenes. BRAVO principals do this because it empowers others, it makes them look even better, but more than that... it is the right thing to do.

Share Power
with the Larger Community

When the community feels a valued part of the school leadership, there is a strong buy-in to the needs of the school and the important role this plays for the community itself. I am reminded of the recent school bond election that occurred in one of our urban cities. The district was desperately in need of a new high school facility. Community businesses and senior citizen groups did not understand these needs, and, because there was no relationship with school leaders, there was no community leadership in support of the bond. Sure enough, when the election was held the school bond was defeated. Two years later, the bond issue came up again on the ballot. This time it passed. What had changed? Under the leadership of a new superintendent, community members had been invited into the school and school/business partnerships had been forged emphasizing mentoring programs and service learning. In other words, new relationships were being created every day, built with actions that said "our community school values your leadership."

Share Power with Students

This idea of nurturing leadership at every level, or "capacity building" as Lambert (2003) calls it, is important for students also. In fact, if a major goal of schools is to prepare students to live in a democracy, and most of us would say that this is so, then it is imperative that students be empowered to learn how to exercise power responsibly. Consider your schools for a moment. Are your student councils and class officers being provided with leadership training? They should be. Principals who build relationships with actions that value others empower through developing leadership at all levels of the school.

Tactical Actions
that Empower Others

Recently I attended a meeting of university professors. Leading our meeting was a semi-retired professor who had been teaching leadership for many years. It seemed that every phrase he uttered was rich with wisdom, and he prefaced many of his statements with, "Now, this is what my teacher told me. ..." As he began to talk about carrying out the shared vision of an organization, he said, "My teacher told me to never use the word 'activities,' but to use 'tactics' instead." Activities are too often without direction and too frequently become busy work, but the very term 'tactics' implies purposeful intent. So, what tactical actions can BRAVO principals implement to empower others?

- Listen actively.
- Remind faculty why they became educators.
- Involve all stakeholders in creating the campus vision for student success.
- Develop a collaborative plan that clearly articulates objectives and strategies for implementing the campus vision.
- Establish collaborative procedures to assess and modify plans to ensure achievement of the campus vision and then implement them.
- Acknowledge and celebrate the contributions of all stakeholders toward realization of the campus vision publicly and privately.
- Communicate effectively with all groups in the school and the community, the powerful and the seemingly powerless.
- Promote continuous academic, social, and emotional development of all students.
- Say what you mean and mean what you say.
- Do what you say you will do.
- Trust the judgment of others.
- Give teachers the freedom to teach.

- ◆ Convey your trust in parents by providing mean-ingful opportunities for them to be engaged in their children's education.
- ◆ Involve others in decision making.
- ◆ Recognize leadership throughout your campus.
- ◆ Delegate responsibly.
- ◆ Use follow-up procedures to support staff.
- ◆ Establish partnerships with parents, businesses, and others in the community to strengthen pro-grams and support campus goals.

When the school community actively participates to-gether to create a vision shared by all, when leaders are will-ing to trust the wisdom and experience of others, when lead-ership is recognized and developed at every level, leaders ac-tively demonstrate their belief in empowerment. However, believing in the concept of empowerment is not enough. Turn-ing this belief into an action happens only when school lead-ers give their power away and share it with others. The very act of empowering others builds and enhances relationships grounded in valuing others.

Remember, BRAVO principals build relationships with actions that value others through Empowering.

Empowering Actions

- ■ Create a Shared Vision
- ■ Restore the Vision
- ■ Frame the Vision around Student Success
- ■ Establish Trust
- ■ Give Teachers the Freedom to Teach
- ■ Delegate Responsibly
- ■ Build Leadership at Every Level
- ■ Share Power with Teachers
- ■ Share Power with the Larger Community
- ■ Share Power with Students

2

Actions that Are Supportive: Lighten the Load

"No one is useless in this world who lightens the burdens of another."

Charles Dickens
(Peter, 1977, 440)

Early toward the beginning of my teaching career, I worked for an elementary principal who considered it his primary responsibility at the school to "lighten the load" of the teachers and free us up to teach our very best. No matter how early I got to school, he was always there, and usually walking the halls. As he passed each classroom, he looked in and said with a cheery smile (I never understood how he managed that so early in the morning), "How can I help you today?" I always responded with a nod and said, "Oh, nothing, thank you, I've got everything under control." He would walk on to the next room, look in, and greet that teacher in the same way.

One morning, I was running really late and arrived at school just a few minutes before the students arrived. As I rushed to my classroom, I saw the principal standing at my door. I could not believe my bad luck. Just as I opened my mouth to explain what had happened to make me so late, he said, "It looks as though you have gotten off to a very rough start today. There must be something that I can do for you this morning to lighten your load?" Then, he actually took the ditto masters that were in my hand (yes, this was in the day of the purple mimeograph machines) and brought classroom copies to my door several minutes later—with a smile. Later, I realized that he never asked, nor did I ever tell him, why I was so late to school that morning. This happened a long time ago and I have worked with many principals since that time, and though I no longer remember his name, when I think about principals whose supportive actions model valuing the faculty, I always see his face.

Principals who "lighten the burden" show their care and concern for teachers and students alike, but it transcends the workplace. Principals who build relationships with actions that value others must certainly be aware of what is happening professionally on their campuses, but they must also be sensitive to what is happening personally. To do this they must communicate effectively, offer encouragement, and recognize needs.

Support Through Communicating Effectively

There is no doubt that effective communication by principals positively influences faculty and students and encourages them to feel supported. In fact, Verdugo and Schneider (1999) studied the characteristics of quality schools and safe schools, and open communication ranked among the top five traits these schools had in common. Supportive communicative behaviors emphasize being available, listening actively, and having a communication plan.

Be Available

Effective principals both talk with and listen to students and faculty to learn about them as individuals. After all, the students who are in our classrooms and the staff with whom we work are not just student and staff. They are multidimensional: son, daughter, cousin, friend, parent, brother, sister, grandparent, artist, athlete, and so much more. We can get a glimpse of who these people really are only by making ourselves available to see them and hear them in an authentic manner.

To gain better glimpses of faculty and students while I was principal, I would arrive at school early, stay late, and attempt to be in the halls as much as possible. This often provided me with private glimpses into the lives of staff and students. It was during these times that I learned that a teacher's husband had just lost his job, that another teacher was having marital difficulties, and that a young teacher, newly married and with a baby, was having serious financial difficulties. I saw high school boyfriends and girlfriends break up and knew that a well-placed word to a teacher might help ease the stress of their teenage unhappiness. I noticed which students always seemed to be alone, without friends, or were struggling to make connections in the school.

I remember a middle school student, an only child who was new to our school. His name was Jason and every time I saw him—in the halls, or outside waiting for his ride—he stood or sat alone. I began to look for him in the cafeteria. If he sat at lunch with others, he always sat on the perimeter, and, though he listened to the conversations around him, I never saw him take part. I began to engage him in conversation and, within a few days, discovered that he loved to draw and was very good. Before too long, when he saw me, he would approach with his notebook open to show me his latest drawing. When he left mid-year to move to another state, there was a folder in my office of drawings that said, "To my friend, from Jason."

To increase availability, many principals have an open door policy. This means that teachers and students can go to the principal and share their concerns without feeling threatened. One teacher described her principal's availability as, "We can agree to disagree. Once, I had a problem where she [the principal] promoted an aide in my department without telling me. I felt that I could ask her about it and I did. The principal said, 'Sorry, but that was my call.'" The teacher then added, "But, she didn't hold it against me for asking about it and I felt supported just because I knew that I could talk to her."

Teachers are much more likely to share a personal problem that might be affecting their teaching when the principal is accessible. I've known many principals over the years whose teachers have come to the office, closed the door, and told of financial problems, babysitter problems, marital woes, and illnesses in the family. In almost every case, principals appreciate the confidences because it helps them be supportive in a more directed way. I know of principals who have helped spouses find jobs, located child care, recommended marriage counselors, and even arranged doctor appointments. One principal took a new teacher, who was on a very tight budget, shopping. They bought several dress jackets in different colors, to help her dress more professionally.

I am not advocating that *social worker* be added to the principal's job description. Certainly it is true that principals walk a fine line when involving themselves in the personal lives of staff and students. But the reality is that when principals are visible and available to staff and students, relationships are built, and acknowledging personal stresses of staff and students is necessary to support the growth of the school. In schools where principals develop relationships that value others, the personal and professional lives will sometimes overlap.

Listen Actively

One of the most important components of good communication is the ability to listen actively. This creates a warm, friendly environment. Throughout the school day, principals have many opportunities, formally and informally, to listen. Principals will not *find* time to listen, so they must *make* time. One way that principals model active listening is to put their pencil down or turn away from the computer screen, and look at the speaker and really listen. On the other hand, there is no quicker way to make one feel of no value than to say, while continuing to work: "Go ahead, I'm listening." Who can communicate effectively to the back of someone's head? One might as well say to the speaker: "You are not important enough for me to listen to you." Certainly, busy principals are often overwhelmed with deadlines, and there are times when one just cannot listen properly. When this happens, it is much better to admit, "You know, I really want to hear what you have to say, but I have to complete this project right now. Could you come back in 10 minutes?"

Another way that a principal demonstrates active listening is by restating what has just been said. For example, after listening to a teacher or student or parent, the principal might respond, "So what you're telling me is. ..." This clarifies the discussion and prevents misunderstandings. It also says to the speaker that the principal values the communication so much that she not only wants to listen, but also wants to understand.

Recently, in a conversation in one of my principal classes a student shared this example of listening actively. It was two days before school was scheduled to start and the building that was supposed to have been completed in July, still was not quite ready for students. At least that was the teachers' opinion. However, the superintendent had decided that the building was ready enough and school would start on time. He had also emphasized that teachers could not rely on maintenance help as they would be busy with other last-minute building preparations. As the principal and teachers were frantically completing at least a million details to prepare for that first day, the principal met a young first-year teacher in the hall. Hurriedly, he said, "How is everything going?" She responded, "I think I would be just fine, if I only had a pencil sharpener!" He made no comment and walked on.

The next morning, before leaving for school, the principal went into the garage, found his toolbox and took it to work. When the young teacher walked into her room that morning, there he was, dressed in suit and tie, wrestling with a screw driver as he installed her pencil sharpener. Now, that's active listening!

Have a Communication Plan

Good communication does not happen by accident. In fact, communication often suffers because the job of the principal is so busy and so fragmented. However, principals with a specific communication plan are able to provide needed support that leads to effective relationship building.

For example, because teachers are so busy, a principal who is organized and makes good use of faculty meeting times clearly nurtures and sustains relationships that value others. The best principal communicator that I know only has one or two faculty meetings a year, and these meetings always have a carefully constructed agenda with beginning and ending times. She makes regular use of several other communication strategies, such as e-mail, and provides everyone with a weekly calendar that includes planned information about what will be happening on campus that week. This busy principal encourages regular department or grade level meetings, but even these meetings are required to follow an agenda and a time frame. At the beginning of each school year, she reiterates to the faculty how important they are to the school and notes that busy people just do not have time to waste. Rather than sitting in meetings, their job is to be about "helping students and doing great things for this campus."

Support Through Offering Encouragement

Offering encouragement is an important action that builds relationships that value others. A quick e-mail to a teacher or a student from the principal acknowledging a noticed extra effort is like the veritable shot in the arm. It reenergizes, renews commitment, and builds relationships that contribute to a strong sense of community.

Provide Informal Encouragement

As a professor at a regional university, many of my principal preparation classes are held in public schools in the late afternoon. This provides a wonderful opportunity to observe principals and assistant principals interacting with those few students who always seem to linger after school has been dismissed. In fact, one principal told me recently, "I think the most important time of the day for me is after school when the halls and classrooms are almost empty, but not quite. That's when I have a chance to engage a student in real conversation, and sometimes I find some very interesting, occasionally disturbing, things about my kids." He then told how last year he had visited with a student who was struggling academically. In their conversation, the student shared that he was working two part-time jobs in the evening and sometimes did not get off work until well after midnight. The principal made some phone calls and found the student a better paying job that allowed him to be home each evening before 9 p.m. In no time, the student's grades improved. This act not only encouraged the student, but emphasized support of the individual as well as the academic process.

Encourage New Teachers

The literature today is full of stories of new teachers who leave teaching after only one year because it is such a difficult, stressful job. Within four years, 25 percent of all beginning teachers leave the profession, and for schools in high-poverty areas the statistics are even greater (Hare & Heap, 2001a, 2001b). Awareness of this has led many principals to be extra sensitive to the need to encourage new faculty members. They place notes in their boxes when they see them do something well. When looking at lesson plans, principals are careful to make positive comments. The first year that I taught, my principal invited new teachers to a sandwich lunch. He did this every year to remind teachers to "sandwich" their comments to parents and students—make a positive comment, next point out an area that needs improvement (stated very tactfully, of course), then make another positive comment. This sandwich principle is a valuable way to support and encourage both faculty and students.

Mentor New Teachers

Another way to encourage new teachers is through mentoring. Teachers new to the profession say that being involved in a mentoring program has provided encouragement in a variety of ways, such as by becoming more familiar with the curriculum, by strengthening classroom management skills, and by helping them feel a part of the school. It is especially in this "feeling a part of the school" that building relationships with teachers and students can begin.

When we started a mentor program at one school, participating teachers kept a journal. As I read through the journals at the end of their first year, I was struck by the number of times I saw the word "encourage." One new teacher wrote, "My mentor teacher encourages me every day by being available when I need her to listen to my fears. While she always reminds me that I can do this, she usually gives me a little helpful tip that makes this possible!" Another new teacher commented, "I would never have survived this first year without my mentor. I had forgotten how teenagers could be such a challenge, until my mentor teacher encouraged me to remember what I was like as a teenager … yes, I can do this!" A mentor program is often the first step for new teachers to move beyond mere survival. Invariably, quality mentor encouragement helps new teachers focus on their goal of becoming that person they wanted to be: someone who helps kids.

Encourage Master Teachers

It is not enough for principals to see that new teachers are encouraged. What do we do for our master teachers? Master teachers know the curriculum, they have honed their delivery skills to an art, their students and parents love them, and other teachers on the faculty see them as a resource. In fact, when there is a committee that needs to be led, a topic that needs to be researched, or any job that needs to be done, principals call on the master teacher. At least, I did. Then one day, one of our experienced, most respected teachers walked into my office, shut the door, and resigned. Just like that! As she left the office that day, her words rang in my ear, "I used to love teaching. I used to just feel good when I drove onto this campus, but now I am so busy being on committees, so busy doing paper work, that I don't even have time to get to know my students, let alone the other teachers. I haven't heard a word of encouragement in ages!" She was simply burned out! And I had let it happen.

I had assumed that this experienced, admired teacher received all the encouragement she needed just by being recognized as a leader on campus, and I felt that my words of encouragement were not necessary. I was so wrong! I thought I was building leadership capacity, but this teacher perceived it as assigning extra work. Assigning extra work is not the same as providing encouragement to an excellent teacher for a job well done. In order for principals to build relationships with actions that value others, we must remember to encourage *everyone* on the campus.

Support Through Recognizing Needs

For a principal to recognize needs within the school, he must know the teachers and the students. Once again, this reaches beyond the professional and into the personal lives of faculty and students. Principals who focus on building relationships that value others know faculty and students so well that they often recognize needs because of the visible changes that take place. BRAVO principals also acknowledge that teachers and students have personal demands on them that are outside the realm of the school.

Know Faculty and Students Well

During my years as an educator, I have worked with many outstanding principals and teachers. I remember one experience in particular. Jane was always on time, she turned all paperwork in when it was due, her lesson plans were thorough, she was always willing to volunteer for extra duties, she prepared interesting, challenging lessons, and she communicated with parents well. Then everything changed. Jane was occasionally late to school, she quit volunteering, she began losing weight, she often appeared absent-minded, and students complained about boring lectures.

One late afternoon the principal walked by Jane's classroom and saw her sitting at her desk just staring at a pile of papers stacked in front of her. The principal stood for a moment, silently watching, expecting her to begin grading the papers. But she did not. Instead, she simply sat motionless, with pencil in hand. Finally, the principal cleared her throat and spoke. They chatted for a few minutes, then the principal commented that she had noticed a change lately, and asked if there were anything she could do. Hesitantly, Jane began telling about her husband of 30 years who had recently announced that he no longer wanted to be married and had moved out. The principal and the teacher talked for quite awhile. Then Jane remarked, "You know, it actually feels good to talk about this." She thanked the principal for *noticing her need*. While, it did not happen overnight, before too long, she was once again a teacher-leader at the school.

Acknowledge Personal Issues

One of my graduate students actually transferred schools because her former principal had been so uncaring about personal issues that she became physically nauseated if she had to ask to take off early or call in due to one of her children's illnesses. She now teaches at a school with an exemplary rating where the principal acknowledges the need for family to come first. Her new principal tells teachers at the beginning of the school year that she understands the importance of family and, though she expects teachers to put forth 110 percent effort at school, she also understands their need to be able to attend their own children's field trips, take sick children to the doctor, even go away for a few vacation days with a husband. To make hard-working teachers feel less guilty when they must ask for a day off, she reminds them, "After all, good teachers should role model being good parents."

Principals are not expected to answer every need that arises for faculty and students, especially those that arise due to personal issues. But BRAVO principals know that to acknowledge these needs exist is an important way to demonstrate support. I have a principal friend who consistently reminds teachers that "there is more to that student sitting in front of you than paper and pencil." In other words, look beyond the assignments to better understand a student. For the faculty, this principal openly acknowledges that she knows there is "more to your life than what goes on at school." Often, just a simple acknowledgment of the complexities of balancing the professional life with the personal life is support enough to encourage others.

Support Through Providing Resources

The next logical step after recognizing needs is providing resources, yet many principals never take this step. Principals who value others recognize needs and do something to meet those needs in a variety of ways.

Make Time in the School Day

Generally, when we think of providing resources we focus primarily on locating money, which is, of course, critical. But time is a tremendous resource, and principals who value others look for ways to structure the school day to provide time for planning and thinking. An elementary school was in the midst of changing curriculum from a phonics reading program to a whole language program. There was much discussion because it was not just the program that was changing, but teacher philosophies of reading were undergoing much change. This principal provided the resource of time within the school day; time for teachers to read and learn what the research had to say about both approaches to reading; time for faculty to plan together to identify ways to bring about needed changes; and time to practice implementing these changes.

Other schools have experimented with creative scheduling, such as having different grade levels start school at different times on a rotating schedule and allowing for grade level teams to meet and plan together. Schools have used teacher aides and, sometimes, trained parent volunteers to monitor classes while teachers plan together. Many principals have noted that they use faculty meetings as professional development opportunities, and use e-mail and newsletters to communicate information that used to be shared in faculty meetings. One principal trained the school's teachers AND three instructional aides in the use of new computer software. When it was time for the teachers to use the software, the aides were available and knowledgeable in providing support help during the school day. Many of the teachers commented later that even though they had gone to the computer training, it was not until they sat down with the instructional aides one-on-one and put the software to use, that it all made sense. Principals acknowledge the wise use of time when they provide much-needed support.

Of course, students and learning should always be the number one most important priority of the school, but when principals structure the school day so that teachers can plan together, learn together, and, engage in collaborative reflection, students can remain the priority. Time is a major resource and BRAVO principals plan the activities of the school day in such a way that they make the very best use of time.

Identify Resources Creatively

Good principals notice when teachers are struggling with limited resources in the classroom and they find ways to fulfill needs. Several students in my principal preparation classes have shared that their principals suggest they do their major research paper on a topic that can be turned into a grant proposal. Now when I introduce the research classes to my students, I also suggest they consider some of the needs at their school, and structure their research papers around those needs with the goal in mind of using their research papers as foundations for grant proposals. Several of these have been successful, and the schools have obtained valuable grant monies to provide resources for after-school tutoring programs, service-learning projects, and other areas of need.

One of the challenges for a principal who spear-headed a reading change on campus was to allocate funds to purchase trade books. There was no money in the budget, so he organized and publicized a community-wide book fair; even the mayor came to read with the students one day. This activity filled the classrooms with trade books for the children to read.

Principals who identify needs and then brainstorm with teachers and students encourage creative ways to provide classroom resources, especially in these tight budget times. I am reminded of the day a principal observed in an art class and casually remarked that the students' work was so good, it really should be for sale. About a week later, art students came to her and asked if they could have a show and sell their work to interested patrons to raise money to buy a kiln for the art department. How could she say no?

Tactical Actions that Support Others

How can BRAVO principals build relationships that value others through supportive actions?

- ♦ Be visible in the halls and in the classrooms.
- ♦ Be approachable.
- ♦ Keep a pleasant demeanor (smile).
- ♦ Be a good listener.
- ♦ Make time to listen.

- Clarify what is said to be sure the understanding is clear.
- Offer encouragement privately and publicly.
- Recognize students and teachers for a job well done through notes, bulletin boards, newsletters, etc.
- Go the extra mile for others.
- Offer help when it is needed.
- Notice changes that occur in individuals.
- Draw from a variety of information sources to notice needs.
- Provide resources of time, as well as supplies and finances.
- Provide training for staff to ensure that all students are provided high-quality, flexible instructional programs with necessary resources.
- Learn how to obtain grant resources.
- Diagnose campus climate and faculty and student morale through informal discourse.
- Diagnose school climate through the use of surveys and focus groups.
- Provide ongoing support to campus staff.
- Use other people's time wisely.
- Respond to social and economic issues in the school environment and beyond.

If I were standing in front of the ancient Arizona cliff dwelling that I mentioned earlier with a container of red paint in my hand, I know exactly what I would draw to symbolize the role of a principal who is supportive of the faculty. I would draw an inverted pyramid with the principal on the bottom point, and teachers and students all along the top. The principal is the supporting influence that enables the work of the school to be productive. Even more, when the principal models this level of support, it becomes contagious and others support one another in the same manner.

A supportive principal becomes a servant of the school. Principals support the building of relationships by communicating wisely, by encouraging others, by recognizing needs, and by providing resources to enhance the quality of school life, as well as personal lives. When principals' actions are supportive, faculty and students feel valued. We have all heard the story of the two bricklayers working side by side. One was asked what he was doing and he responded, "I'm laying bricks." The other was asked the same question. He responded, "I'm building a cathedral." Good principals don't just work at a school, instead, by providing support, they work at building people.

Remember, BRAVO principals build relationships with actions that value others through being Supportive.

Supportive Actions

Communicate Effectively

- Be Available
- Listen Actively
- Have a Communication Plan

Offer Encouragement

- Provide Informal Encouragement
- Encourage New Teachers
- Mentor New Teachers
- Encourage Master Teachers

Recognize Needs

- Know Faculty and Students Well
- Acknowledge Personal Issues

Provide Resources

- Make Time in the School Day
- Identify Resources Creatively

3

Actions that Are Respectful: Make People Feel Important

"Everyone has an invisible sign hanging from his neck saying 'Make Me Feel Important!' Never forget this message when working with people."

Mary Kay Ash
(Safire & Safir, 1990, p. 168)

It was the last day of the school year and, as far as I was concerned, my first and last year of being a principal at this school. When I accepted the assignment, I knew there was a very bad morale problem at the school, not just with faculty, but with students and parents as well. So, I had determined that I would be open to new ideas and that together we would build a school community that was positive and affirming for everyone on campus. And we had tried all kinds of new ideas: *implemented new scheduling* in the high school, *reviewed new curriculum*, all faculty meetings had a time for open sharing, and I had even taken seniors to lunch off campus in small groups in an effort to understand their needs better. But still there was grumbling. May 29 was finally here; I was exhausted, as was the faculty. But, I had one last meeting to chair.

I entered the classroom with my yellow pad in hand and turned to face a tired faculty. "Now, let's talk about this past year. What worked and what did not work," I said. Immediately it seemed as though the room was energized. Teachers spoke out, some raised their hands, and, with my assistant's help, we copied down every negative comment. We would have noted the positive ones, but there were too few. I made no excuses. I just listened to each comment and wrote it down. An hour later, when the barrage of criticism stopped, I thanked them for their comments, noted that we would evaluate everything very carefully, and wished them a happy summer. Then, I walked straight to my office, closed the door, and sat down and cried. I had tried so hard, but this was not worth it, no way! This was principal abuse!

In about ten minutes, I heard a knock on my office door and in walked five or six of the teachers who had been at the meeting. *They* were smiling and looking absolutely jubilant! "Wow," they said in unison, "what a meeting. That was awesome! Up until this year, no one has ever listened to us, or even acted interested in our input. All year long, we thought this 'new direction' was just temporary, until you got comfortable being principal. Now, we see, you really do care what we think, you do value our expertise, you respect us as teachers, wow!" They turned and left. I stayed for 12 more years!

Treating everyone on the campus with respect is an important way to build relationships that demonstrate how much we value those with whom we work. James Burns wrote, "In real life, the most practical advice for leaders is not to treat pawns like pawns, nor princes like princes, but all people like *people*" (Safire & Safir, 1990, p. 202). In other words, we should treat people the way we would like to be treated. Treating others respectfully means that principals must be fair, they must show by their actions that they care, and they must acknowledge and celebrate diversity. Yet, this simple idea of treating others with respect is often very difficult for leaders to do.

Respect by Being Fair

When principals get together, they immediately begin talking about the challenges of their job. Repeatedly, I hear them discuss a major challenge—how to do the right thing while treating others fairly. Part of this dilemma occurs because we often confuse the concept of fairness with treating everyone the same. Just what is involved in the concept of treating everyone fairly?

Understand What "Fair" Means

The classic example of the concept of fairness often centers around the student in special education who requires modifications to the curriculum due to the nature of the learning disability, such as longer testing times. Invariably, some faculty member will say, "We don't do that for the other students." In this situation, principals can simply remind teachers that following the IEP is required by law.

However, principals who value others want teachers, as well as students and parents, to understand what fair really means and what it does *not* mean. Fair does *not* mean treating everyone exactly the same. For example, some of us are near-sighted. To compensate we wear glasses with corrective lenses. If fair meant treating everyone the same, no one would wear glasses, or everyone would wear glasses.

A few years ago, I knew a delightful student named John who could talk knowledgeably about a wide array of topics and, after just a brief conversation with him, I always walked away thinking how bright he was. John's class work, however, was often minimal, and he was frequently kept in from recess to redo work or complete late assignments. His grades were marginal. "If he would just work harder," was a frequent lament from certain teachers. Some of his teachers, beginning during his elementary school years, had noted that he should be evaluated for a learning disability. Still other teachers, as well as his parents, were adamant that he was just "lazy" and should be treated "like everyone else."

John's dream was to go to a top-tier university. As a junior, he took the SAT and scored in the low 900s. He was crushed; how could he get into the university of his dreams with that score? Finally, he agreed to undergo testing and, just as some of us had expected, he was diagnosed with a learning disability. One of the recommendations was to provide him with academic adjustments, such as longer testing times. John retook the SAT and scored 1400! If fair meant that everyone should be treated the same, John would never have had the opportunity to excel.

Meet Needs

The concept of fair is about meeting individual needs; it is not about treating everyone the same! Principals whose actions are intent on building relationships that value others must consider their faculty and students in each circumstance as they ponder the idea of fairness. This is often complex, for no principal will be respected if he treats people arbitrarily with complete disregard to policy. We all know of principals who let their favorite teachers get by with coming in late or leaving early, or who ignore the misdeeds of a board member's son or daughter, while following "the book" with others. So, what is fair? Let's take a little test.

The school policy says that teachers must be in the classroom 15 minutes before class begins. A young teacher's husband who has always taken the children to preschool on his way to work has been called away at the last minute by the National Guard. The preschool is across town and the teacher is unable to get to school the requisite 15 minutes before class starts. What should a principal do?

A. Put daily notes in the teacher's box reminding her of the school policy to be on time.

B. Document the teacher's lateness and put a memo in her personnel file about being late.

C. Call the teacher in for a conference and tell her that you understand her predicament, but the other teachers must be on time and everyone must be treated the same. She must be on time.

D. Call the teacher in for a conference. She explains what has happened and says that she is talking with a nearby preschool, but they have no openings until next month. The principal assigns an aide to be in her class every morning when needed until she is able to work out a placement for her children.

Of course, D is the best example of an action that values others—it implies respect for the teacher and a willingness to treat this situation with fairness.

To treat people fairly, a principal must understand the situation in all of its complexity. Then principals must do what is best for those involved within the framework of the school's mission. Fair is about meeting individual needs, not about treating everyone the same. Treating others fairly reinforces the action that people are more important than policies. Policies should support the work of the school and the people who work there, but when they do not, principals must have some "wiggle room" to individualize decisions that treat others fairly.

Respect by Caring

The concept of caring about teachers and students goes far beyond what we typically think of as caring. Certainly it means treating others as we like to be treated, being kind, and exhibiting compassion. But caring also means that students and teachers in our schools are challenged to continue growing personally and professionally by the actions of the principal. In fact, the ethic of care is so important that Sergiovanni (1992) pointed out that it is key to academic success.

Nurture Growth

Laurie was in her early 40s, but this was only her second year of teaching. In August, just before school started, the principal's secretary telephoned to say that she could come by and pick up her class list. Excited about her second year after a wonderful first-year experience, Laurie hurried to school to view her third-grade class list. Thirty minutes later she sat in the principal's office and wiped the tears from her eyes. "I can't believe you are putting Tommy [a seriously handicapped child] in my class. This will ruin everything. I am sure that he is a sweet child, but he cannot read at all, he has outbursts of temper, and he is confined to a wheelchair. How can I teach him, I don't know how!" The principal considered before he spoke, then he gently reminded Laurie that perhaps this child was in her room to be taught, but also to be a teacher. He also assured her that he would be there to support her and help her with school resources. Laurie listened, feeling ashamed of her outburst. She left the office and vowed to do her best, even though she seriously doubted that anything good would come from this situation.

At the end of the school year, Laurie made an appointment to see the principal. In his office, she took out a notebook and began to read from her notes:

♦ Tommy clearly loves being in my class. He smiles his crooked smile, but his eyes just light up when I come into the class room.

- Last week I assigned Mary (who is always in trouble for talking, being out of her chair, etc.) to be Tommy's helper. This has worked very well. Now, instead of bothering those who sit near her, she gets up and goes to Tommy and offers to help however she can. I'm seeing a whole new side of Mary.

- Other children in the room are volunteering to be Tommy's helper.

- The class as a whole is very aware of Tommy, but in a good way. Yesterday, when Tommy had a temper tantrum in the middle of math, another student said, "I think, he's just very frustrated, because it's so hard."

Laurie had filled a notebook of the year's experiences. Originally, she had started keeping the notebook to document the difficulty of having a special needs child in her class, but instead the notebook had become a testimony of the value—for her, for her class, and for Tommy—of the importance of caring about others. Laurie thanked the principal for caring enough about her as a teacher to help her grow. Principals build relationships with actions that value others when they care enough to see that every child and teacher on the campus has an opportunity to learn and experience success. Even more, people value being appreciated for what they can contribute to learning, and it is through these acts of caring that principals can "encourage the heart ... to carry on" (Kouzes & Posner, 1995, p. 13).

Discipline Wisely

One of the most frustrating functions of a principal is handling disciplinary issues. Whether disciplining students or faculty members, it is never pleasant. Even when dealing with disciplinary issues, however, principals must remember that their actions demonstrate whether they value others or not, and, ultimately, how much they really care about others. When disciplining, a principal must be respectful of others and treat them the way we all like to be treated. This means

treating faculty the way that we like to be treated professionally, treating parents the way we like to be treated as a parent,
and treating children the way that we would like our own
children to be treated.

Many years ago when my daughter was in the second
grade, I taught in the same school she attended. One day I
walked by her room and saw her and a little boy standing at
their desks with their hands covering their faces. The teacher
was at the chalkboard demonstrating a math lesson to the rest
of the class, who were all seated at their desks. I couldn't
imagine why my daughter and this little boy stood at their
desks with their faces covered. I began to walk past the classroom, but I could not. I turned back, went to the classroom
door, and motioned to the teacher. When she came to the door,
I asked her what was happening. She said, "Oh, don't be upset. They were cheating on the spelling test. This is how I am
punishing them."

I took a deep breath. This was her classroom and I was not
the principal. I was just a teacher in the next room. But, this
was my daughter! Even if she had cheated on a test, I could
not believe this was an appropriate way to deal with her misbehavior. I simply said, "Well, I think they have stood long
enough," and walked away with tears flooding my eyes.
Thankfully, the teacher told the children they could be seated.
When school was over that day, my daughter could not talk
about what had happened without crying. I decided then
when children misbehaved the focus should be on assigning
appropriate consequences that would make a statement without causing undue embarrassment or shame. Whether working with students, faculty, or parents, when they make bad decisions they should still be treated with respect because this
demonstrates that we care.

One of the many challenges facing principals is that of
working with teachers to support them in disciplining students in the classroom. How to do this without telling teachers how to run their classroom is not always easy. One year, a
little boy in the first grade was constantly in trouble in the
classroom, on the playground, at music class, or waiting in the
bus line. After being admonished by the teacher, he always

seemed to be sorry and expressed his desire to do better. Paul was an only child and his parents were professionals who had great expectations for him. They soon realized that he was having difficulty at school, so the parents met with the teacher and they explained that they wanted to be told every time he did something wrong. So, nearly every day, the teacher wrote a note to the parents explaining what Paul had done that day that had been inappropriate. Teacher and parents talked on the phone almost every night. But, Paul's behavior only seemed to get worse.

One afternoon the teacher came by the office and asked the principal for help. The principal listened carefully as she detailed the kinds of misbehavior and told him about the notes and phone calls to the parents who were trying diligently to be supportive. "Every time he does something wrong, I write it down, and send the note home to the parents." she explained. The principal looked thoughtful, then said, "Well, Paul certainly knows by now that you care when he behaves badly... does he know that you care about him when he behaves well?" That evening the teacher contacted the parents and they agreed to a new plan for Paul. This time, Paul took a note home at the end of each day detailing his good behavior. Within a week, Paul's behavior began to improve.

There is a popular saying among teachers: "Students don't care what you know until they know that you care." I would modify this to, "No one cares what you say, if your actions don't say that you care."

Respect by Celebrating Diversity

While, we are alike in many ways, we are also unalike in many ways. We look different, we have different talents and abilities, and we have different experiences at school and away from school. We come from homes that are different. We have different understandings about large and small issues. We come from different cultures. Sometimes differences are subtle, but they exist. Recently, an educator who lived the first

25 years of her life in South Africa shared with me that in South Africa one never passes anything to another using the left hand. To do so is a sign of great disrespect. Even now, as a United States citizen for over ten years, she feels guilty when she uses her left hand to pass something. We know that in some cultures children are taught that to look an adult in the face is very disrespectful. Yet, it is not uncommon for us when we work with these very children to say, "Now, look at me."

We value different things. Another friend of mine is from India. In India families get to know neighboring families very well and visit in and out of their homes daily. In the United States he has lived in the same apartment for two years, and he still has no idea who his neighbors are. Another friend from the Ukraine is concerned that teachers in the United States are much too informal with their students.

Certainly, there are many kinds of diversity. Stand in the halls of any school in the United States today and notice the students. Then, notice the faculty and the administrators. You will most likely notice an interesting difference: Though the students are increasingly racially diverse, the faculty has remained predominantly white and mostly female (Melley, 2001). Administrators are even more predominantly white and most are male, especially at the secondary level. This offers a challenge to administrators who are committed to building relationships with actions that demonstrate respect by acknowledging and celebrating the many faces of diversity.

Notice Diversity Involvement on Campus

Increasingly today, schools are looking closely at their diverse student populations and achievement. For example, in Texas, schools report how well students achieve based on state-mandated tests and these results are broken down and analyzed by groups, such as gender, ethnicity, and socioeconomic status. While this is valuable, there are clubs and activities on the campus that report involvement using different criteria. This is why BRAVO principals notice diversity involvement on campus and are alert and sensitive to membership in pep squads, cheerleader squads, athletic teams, honor societies, and other organizations.

What about the very overweight junior girl who sits alone at lunch all of the time? Or the guy in the junior class who is really short, wears glasses, and stutters? Is there someone on the campus who can befriend these young people? In an effort to support all students, many schools have started mentor programs and service projects as part of a graduation requirement. One service project involved high school juniors who visited a home for senior citizens once a month for a year, as a class project. At the end of the year, the sponsoring principal reported that nearly every student considered it a positive experience. But even more powerful than learning to appreciate the elderly, many of the students commented that they had a new respect for some of their peers. It was through this program that students discovered that the overweight girl who sat alone at lunch all of the time, had a nice singing voice, and she was invited to join a jazz choir. The junior boy who stuttered? He wrote music and one day brought his guitar and serenaded the senior citizens with a song he wrote just for them.

One of my aspiring principal students recently asked his high school students to write something about their school. As he read through their responses, he immediately became aware of the disassociation felt by his Hispanic students. The Anglo students began their papers by saying, "In my school, we. ... The Hispanic students' papers began, "In this school, they. ..." He thought about the racial identity of the school and realized that of the over 100 teachers, only 5 or 6 were Hispanic. He immediately went to his principal with an idea. Together, they formed a group of teachers, administrators, counselors, parents, business leaders, and students and called the group "The Hispanic Forum." The group has created a mission, vision, and goals statement with an emphasis on building community within the school. The students in The Hispanic Forum have even organized a series of classes for teachers in Spanish—taught by the students.

Another principal involved his school in a new program called LINC (Learning for Immigrant New Comers), which is designed for students who are recent arrivals to the United States. Generally, the students do not speak English and are not familiar with the U.S. educational system. Too often these immigrant children are confused and even frightened in our schools. The LINC program shelters these students until they become familiar enough with the language and the school culture to be successful on their own.

All too often, children who are different feel that they are unimportant, or as one junior high student said "I feel invisible when I'm at school." It is the responsibility of principals to model acceptance and support of diversity through their own actions. Knowing student names, welcoming parents to the school, visiting in the homes of under-served students—all of these actions acknowledge authentic support and appreciation of differences. Respectful relationships develop as we get to know others and acknowledge their presence, their needs, their individuality, and their importance. BRAVO principals build respect throughout the campus when they encourage faculty and students to see beyond size, skin color, socioeconomic status, physical impairments, language barriers, and other differences.

Integrate Diversity
Throughout the Curriculum

Principals must challenge their faculties to integrate diversity throughout different aspects of the school curriculum. One way to do this is to incorporate in the English program literature by authors who are Hispanic, African American, Native American, Middle Eastern, and others. Other principals involve faculty in evaluating the history texts to include broader historic events, rather than just those that are Eurocentric. Principals model respect for diversity when they engage their faculty in addressing issues of identity so that children have successful role models that represent all ethnic groups. These principals lead book studies that include books, such as:

◆ Nasdijj. (2000). *The blood runs like a river through my dreams*. Boston: Houghton Mifflin.

◆ Kohl, H. (1994). *I won't learn from you*. New York: The New Press.

- Tatum, B. (1997). *Why are all the black kids sitting together in the cafeteria?* New York: Basic Books.
- Delpit, L. (1995). *Other people's children.* New York: The New Press.
- Howard, G. (1999). *We can't teach what we don't know.* New York: Teachers College Press.

Principals who respect faculty and students cannot limit their concern for diversity to ethnicity. They must also be aware of other aspects of diversity, such as young people questioning their sexuality, those who are overweight, and those who have different religious or economic backgrounds. In schools today, many faculty and students come to school more aware of how they are different than how they are alike. Principals who are concerned about building relationships with actions that value others show their respect by seeing beyond differences to seeing people; they notice the level of engagement of all students and faculty on their campus, and they ensure that the curriculum celebrates diverse heritages. Beyond acknowledging and celebrating diversity, they simply acknowledge and celebrate people.

Tactical Actions that Respect Others

What do BRAVO principals do to model treating others with respect?

- Give faculty and students an opportunity to have input into school policies and procedures.
- Publicly and privately acknowledge faculty and student contributions.
- Commit to seeing that all children on campus have an equal opportunity to experience success.
- Notice the level of involvement of students and faculty.
- Seek the best solution, not always the easiest, when problems occur.
- Spend time with faculty and students.

- When disciplining, assign consequences consistent with the misdeed. Show displeasure for the misdeed; show courtesy to the offender.
- Do what they say they will do
- Listen to what is being said.
- Know people's names.
- Acknowledge faculty and students in the halls, on the grounds, whenever they see them.
- Participate in helping students and faculty members find solutions to personal and professional problems when the opportunity arises.
- Ensure that diversity is integrated throughout the curriculum.
- Invite guest speakers into the school who are representative of diversity.
- Be sensitive to language barriers.
- Challenge faculty to continue learning about students and each other.
- Involve faculty in a book study that focuses on diversity.
- Create a campus where everyone feels welcome.
- Invite parents and community members into the school.
- Treat others the way you would like to be treated.
- Are visible in the community.

To build relationships with actions that value others, principals must be fair, they must be caring, and they must acknowledge and celebrate diversity. In short, they must treat all people in ways that make them feel important.

Remember, BRAVO principals build relationships with actions that value others through being Respectful.

Respectful Actions

Are Fair

- Understand What "Fair" Means
- Meet Needs

Care

- Nurture Growth
- Discipline Wisely

Celebrate Diversity

- Notice Diversity Involvement on Campus
- Integrate Diversity throughout the Curriculum

4

Actions that Challenge the Imagination: Think Creatively

"Where all men think alike, no one thinks very much."

Walter Lippmann
(Peter, 1977, p. 469)

"It is not best that we should all think alike; it is difference of opinion which makes horse races."

Mark Twain
(Peter, 1977, p. 469).

Nature sometimes gives us powerful examples of how to live our lives as busy school principals. This happened a few years ago when my husband and I stood over a small stream at Lake Tahoe and watched the salmon return to their birthplace. It was not pleasant to watch. These once pale salmon were now bright red as they swam furiously, paddling, jumping, and pushing their way against the upstream current. They were using every ounce of their energy to return home where they would bury their eggs in the stream bed and then die. How depressing and sad, I thought at first. Then I had another visual image. In a few weeks, this very stream would burst with thousands of tiny salmon who would join the flowing stream and begin a new life downstream. Every adult salmon that had made that painful, energy-consuming swim upstream to deposit eggs had challenged the imagination and had, ultimately, provided a creative new life force. But it was not an easy task.

Fortunately, the upstream swim for principals is not so tragic, but I think this illustrates how very difficult the role of the principal is as she establishes and nurtures a school climate that can grow by challenging the imagination. In fact, it is the very act of encouraging faculty, students, and their parents to think outside the box that creates much of the conflict surrounding the principalship today. How a principal handles creativity that leads to successful change on a campus, how a principal leads the school in solving problems, and how a principal handles conflict are key ingredients to a principal's success in building relationships among campus stakeholders that value others.

Challenge the Imagination
When Bringing about Change

Being able to bring change to a campus when it is needed is a valuable leadership skill. I am reminded of a school leader who proudly proclaimed to anyone who would listen that he was a change agent. True, he was a talented educator. He knew curriculum strategies and the importance of obtaining resources for schools. He knew powerful people and often could pick up the telephone and solve a resource problem almost instantly. He was a voracious reader who could quote from Aristotle, Plato, and Socrates. He kept up with modern readings and knew the most recent education research and best practices for schools. As a principal, he usually spent no more than three years at a campus. Typically, he came to a new campus, diagnosed its problems, implemented changes, and left for another school. At the next school, he followed the same routine. He built few relationships with staff members or the community. But he did bring change to the campus and some of the changes were good ones. He also brought conflict, confusion, and chaos. Furthermore, within a year of his leaving, many of the changes often were forgotten (including the good ones), and everything was back to the way it had been before he had come only now sometimes things were worse.

To create a climate within our schools that fosters successful change that leads to student success, principals must consider factors that include (Harris & Lowery, 2003):

   ♦ Creating a culture that is supportive and inviting for the learning community

   ♦ Establishing collaborative leadership

   ♦ Clarifying student-centered accountability strategies

   ♦ Encouraging teachers to commit to a care ethic

At the same time, principals must be aware that even the best researched change strategy will likely fail when we do not acknowledge that change is about people.

Acknowledge that Change Is about People

While initiating change on a campus is valuable, being able to nurture and sustain that change is equally or, perhaps, an even more important role for a principal. Recognizing the importance of valuing the people who will be most affected by the changes and involving them in designing and implementing change are key to bringing effective change to a campus that results in successful, long-term experiences for everyone.

Bringing about change in a school goes beyond policies, procedures, curriculum, and other school issues. Change is accomplished by individuals and is highly personal. It involves developmental growth; therefore, the focus should be on individuals not on programs. For example, teachers involved in implementing change are often at different stages of professional growth. New teachers may embrace change eagerly, while older, more experienced teachers may be perfectly happy just the way things are. Or, in your school, it may be just the other way around. New teachers may be so concerned with just trying to survive that the idea of change is unbearable, while experienced teachers are eager for change. James Burns emphasized the "people-aspect" of change when he wrote, "The ultimate test of practical leadership is the realization of intended, real change that meets people's enduring needs" (Burns, 1978, p. 461).

Involve Stakeholders in School Change

Before I became an elementary principal, I had been a reading teacher. I was passionate (and still am) about the importance of children learning to read and loving to read. As a principal supervising teachers, I became more and more aware of the emphasis on skills and decoding, and of phonics being taught in isolation of comprehension at our school. It began to seem as though teaching reading skills and enjoying reading books were separate and unrelated ideas. I believed that reading should be taught in fun and interesting ways, which would result in children knowing how to decode words as well as developing a love for reading.

But what could I do to initiate a reading program change on our campus? Many of our teachers had been teaching only phonics for a long time and were totally committed to this approach to reading. Still others were vigorously opposed to a whole language approach that used trade books (the children called this "real reading") to teach reading. When I first brought up the idea of evaluating our reading curriculum for a possible change, I immediately encountered strong resistance.

Following the advice on change strategies recommended by Hord, Rutherford, Huling-Austin, and Hall (1987), I focused on the need of the children to love reading, and on the teachers who would be able to convey this love through their teaching. Because I valued the teachers involved and trusted their ability to think imaginatively and creatively, we began a dialogue that resulted in an integrated, literature-based reading program with strong components of phonics, decoding skills, comprehension, and reading "real" books. Even the librarian noticed an almost immediate difference in the eagerness of the children to check out books and read them during their library times. Parents, too, began to talk about how their children were far more interested in reading books than they had ever seen them. That year, when we had our annual book fair, more books were purchased by our elementary students than at any school in our city.

Bringing this change in the reading program to our school, was not *my* change. Granted, I had initiated the conversation. But, without involving the faculty, this change would likely never have occurred; and, if it had, without their involvement it would never have lasted. Once the dialogue began, it was the teachers who agreed that they wanted to provide our students with the very best reading program possible. The teachers began to think creatively—they used their imaginations to design a reading program that met an enduring need: teaching children to read in a way that would encourage them to love reading.

Challenge the Imagination
When Solving Problems

Principals face a myriad of problems every day, and sometimes these problems seem insurmountable. In fact, novelist G. K. Chesterton once said, "It isn't that [you] can't see the solution, it's that you can't see the problem" (Peter, 1977, p. 408). Being an imaginative problem solver is just part of the principal's job description.

Use Creative Problem Solving

Hiring staff is always a challenge for principals. One year there were not very many applications to fill the teaching vacancies in a rural school, so the principal hired a young woman, Ms. Smith, who was not a certified teacher, to teach the fourth grade. Her interview with the principal and other staff members had been very impressive, and she seemed to have the requisite understanding of classroom management, child psychology, curriculum, and other related skills that would help her in the classroom.

By early October, the principal realized that there were major problems in Ms. Smith's classroom. She could not discipline the students. She simply "loved them too much." Consequently, even though she had wonderful lesson plans, she could not get through a lesson. The atmosphere in the classroom was completely out of control. Ms. Smith began to develop migraines and so did the principal.

Finally, the principal went to the fourth grade team leader, who had been the first to notice the seriousness of the problem and had asked for ideas. The team leader had already been meeting with Ms. Smith about ways to improve her teaching, but always the conference ended with Ms. Smith saying, "Oh, that's a good idea; yes, I'll do that tomorrow." But somehow, tomorrow never came, or if it did, the chaos in the classroom was so all-consuming that the good idea just could not be implemented.

By mid-October, after numerous conferences, all duly documented, the principal had come to the realization that at the rate things were falling apart in the classroom, this young teacher was going to have to be terminated before Christmas. Then, one morning, the team leader came to her office with a triumphant smile on her face. "I have it!" she said. "The problem is that Ms. Smith has never had the experience of observing for any length of time in a well-run classroom. She has never done student teaching. We need to bring in a master teacher to take over her class while she just observes. Then, once things are restored she needs to student teach with the master teacher slowly moving out of the picture."

Where could they find such a teacher? Where would they find the funds? How would they explain this to parents? What would the other teachers think? They were fresh out of ideas, time, and teachers.

Not ready to give up, together the principal and team leader carefully brainstormed all aspects of the idea, and included Ms. Smith in the discussions. The previous year an excellent, well-loved teacher had resigned because she and her husband were moving and she would have been unable to finish out the school year. They approached her with the idea; she agreed to take over the class and let Ms. Smith observe, and then slowly move the class back under Ms. Smith's leadership. She would not accept any pay (miracles do still exist!). Furthermore, she was well known in the school community so the parents would be pleased (and they were). Other teachers, however, were not as easy to convince, and some even came to the principal upset that this was being done.

Well, to make a long story short, it worked! By December, Ms. Smith was fully in charge of her class, the students were learning, parents were delighted, the substitute master teacher had moved to another state, and the school had a very good, young teacher. Over the next several years, Ms. Smith obtained her state teacher's certificate and earned a master's degree before leaving to start a family.

There was an interesting side note to this creative solution. Other faculty were so impressed with this out-of-the-box thinking and this willingness to seek a win-win solution to a problem that soon a common phrase heard around the school was, "Hey, I've got this idea…"

Navigate Barriers

Another major responsibility facing principals is to find ways around barriers. Generally, this is how we became principals in the first place. Someone noticed that we were very good at getting things done, despite the problems encountered. Yet, I know of one principal who proudly boasted that he was not there to solve other people's problems. Teachers could bring problems into his office, but they "darn well" better leave with them and solve them on their own! Certainly, the principal cannot solve all of the problems of the school, nor should that even be expected. But a principal's willingness to be a problem solver not only helps the school run smoothly, it builds relationships too. Teachers, students, and parents should be able to bring their problems to the principal's office, but it should not become a dumping ground. Instead, after listening and brainstorming together, they should leave the principal's office with ideas and resources that will help them reach positive solutions. Principals who encourage and support creative problem solving nurture a community of problem solvers.

I used to meet every Thursday morning with the administrative team of our school. It was one of my favorite times of the week. As we discussed immediate school problems, we also tried to identify potential issues before they became problems. Sometimes we would bring a problem to the table, sure that there was absolutely no possible solution. But, invariably, as we talked, acknowledged every idea as a possibility, and added our collective imagination to it, we would eventually agree on a possible solution. Many times we implemented a solution, only to revise and refine it over and over in the weeks to come.

Imaginative problem solving is similar to cleaning up a room. The more we clean, the more we notice other things that need to be done. All of a sudden, the cobwebs in the corner become visible, then the cracks in the ceiling become obvious, and on and on. The look of the room improves with each completed task, but the job seems to be never ending. The act of solving problems does not result in a solution that will last forever; instead, it represents a beginning that leads to a better idea, that leads to another idea, and on and on. Imaginative problem solving is not a means to an end, it is a means to a beginning.

Challenge the Imagination
When Managing Conflict

Most principals view conflict as something negative, something to fear. I hate to admit it, but I remember well seeing certain teachers outside my office and wishing that I had a secret exit to the parking lot. I remember how my heart would skip a beat and my palms actually would get sweaty when the administrative assistant would tell me that Mrs. Angry Mother was on the phone. And I can honestly tell you that I never said to anyone while in the midst of conflict, "Wow, this is really an awesome good time!" Conflict is not fun.

Conflict can be positive, however. It can be an inspiring catalyst to thinking creatively. Conflict, when dealt with appropriately, can result in building and bonding a strong community of learners. Accomplishing this result depends on how the principal responds to people who do not agree with each other or with him. Principals who build relationships with actions that value others recognize that thinking alike, while nice, rarely leads to growth.

Listen and Say Little

I learned a valuable strategy for surviving conflict in my first year as a high school principal. One morning I was met at the office door by a father who was absolutely breathing fire! He was furious. His son had not made the varsity basketball team. I've never been a particularly quick thinker on short notice, so unable to put him off, and with no secretary to rescue me, I invited him into my office. I offered him a chair, which he refused to take. For the next 15 minutes, he paced in front of my desk, walking back and forth, making his points about his son's basketball ability, the lack of ability of our coach, the even greater weakness of our school in having a woman principal, who obviously had no control of the coaches and their decisions, and on and on and on.

I picked up a pencil, placed my yellow pad in front of me, and jotted down some of his comments for effect. But I said nothing, other than to nod my head occasionally. I never disagreed with him; I never agreed with him. I simply listened and appeared calm. (Note, I said "appeared.") All of a sudden, he sat down in the chair, looked at his watch, took a deep breath, and said in an amazingly calm voice, "Well, I feel better. I guess I really lost it, didn't I? Thank you for listening. I am so disappointed my son did not make varsity, but he is only a sophomore. And we do like the JV coach. Yes, I think that will be a good experience for him. Well, thanks again for listening. I better get to work."

I stood up at my desk, walked the father to the door, reminded him that my door was always open, and then he was gone. I returned to my desk, dumbstruck. What had just happened? I had been in the midst of conflict and I had survived. By listening, I had acknowledged the conflict; by saying little, I had more than survived, I had made a friend. Weeks later, I ran into this gentleman at a meeting. My instincts said, "run"; once again there was no where to go. He walked up to me with a smile on his face and introduced me to his companion by saying, "This is one brave lady and a great principal!" I smiled and once again said nothing. In the words of Abraham Lincoln, "When you have an elephant by the hind legs and he is trying to run, it's best to let him go" (Dare to Succeed, 1991, p. 210).

Address Problems
Before They Become Conflicts

There are other approaches to conflict in addition to my "listen and say little" strategy. For example, principals can (and should) address potential problems *before* they become full-fledged conflicts. In working at building relationships with teachers, students, and parents, principals often become aware of potential problems during informal conversation. Simply greeting parents, students, or teachers with, "Hi, how are things going for you this year?" can generate important information. A good example of this happened to a principal during a chat with a high school student at the grocery store. She asked how things were going, and he replied, "Fine, I think." When she questioned him further, she discovered that his English teacher had yet to return any graded papers and it was seven weeks into the school year! The next day, the principal visited with the English teacher. She did not immediately accuse her of not grading papers, but in the conversation they brain stormed ways to make English assignments reasonable so the teacher could get them graded in a timely fashion to provide follow-up to the students. About a week later, the principal made a point to see the young man and ask him how things were going in English. His answer was much more definite this time.

Addressing conflict means that as principals we often have to use another "C" word.

Yes, that's right, I said it… confront, confrontation, whatever it takes to address a possible conflict. Confrontation is never fun and we usually try our best to think of ways to solve problems without confronting them head on. However, problems rarely solve themselves. In fact, ignoring problems, usually causes them to just grow… and before you know it, a little smoke has become a raging inferno.

One year, a principal friend hired a brand new History teacher. This new teacher was in his mid-30s and he had previously been a salesman. From the first day, he had problems with discipline in the classroom. He had a quick temper and could not understand why the students did not just hang on his every word. The principal had always prided herself on her tact and the ability to say serious things in the nicest way. And so the principal tried to help this new teacher with classroom management suggestions, but he ignored her advice. Finally, she realized that he was just not hearing what she was saying. Obviously, he felt that her suggestions were just that, suggestions. At last she called him into her office and said, "We have a problem. Your discipline management plan is not working. I am going to give you two ideas that should help. You will implement them both. I will be checking to see that they are in place beginning tomorrow. Any questions?" He stumbled from her office, implemented her suggestions and, you guessed it, things began to improve. By confronting this problem boldly and bluntly, she avoided many potential conflicts with the teacher, students, and parents.

Mediate Conflict
Between Parent and Teacher

Another dilemma that faces principals is dealing with conflict between parent and teacher. Even though schools have a "chain of command," there are instances where the principal must become involved. At the same time, the principal should never put himself between the teacher and the parents in support of one against the other. A principal should support teachers, but this should never be blind support. If a teacher is obviously doing something wrong, the principal has the moral responsibility to work with the teacher to admit the error and work toward resolution. After all, our primary responsibility is to support learning that enables students to be successful.

At a recent focus group meeting, a principal shared this teacher/parent conflict. The teacher had assigned a book report to third graders and had given one of the students an F. The parents tried to contact the teacher, who kept putting off the meeting. Finally, in desperation the parents contacted the principal who told them he would look into it. Upon talking with the teacher, he discovered that there had been no grading rubric, and the directions, by the teacher's own admission, were unclear. She had verbally told the children that the report was to be typed, and this little boy had turned in his paper without typing it. Granted, it was messy and did not deserve an A, but could she justify an F? The principal did not think so. But the teacher was adamant; to change the grade would give in to these parents' demands and where would that lead?

The principal soon realized that the source of the conflict was not so much the grade the teacher had given the student, but her pride in not being able to admit that she might have graded too harshly. After considering his role in helping resolve this conflict, the principal went to the teacher privately and told her that he could not support her decision to give this child an F. At the same time, he also reinforced the many good things she was doing in her classroom. He talked with her about growing from mistakes and asked her what she thought should be done to resolve the situation. With tears in her eyes, the teacher admitted that she needed to reevaluate the child's grade, but she did not want to look ineffective to the parents.

Ultimately, the teacher called the parents for a conference and invited the principal to join them. At the meeting, she told the parents how this situation had caused her to reevaluate the entire project, and she realized there were many ways to make the project better. She asked them for their suggestions to improve the project. At some point during the discussion she agreed that their son's grade should not have been an F and changed it to a C. When it was over, the parents were effusive in their praise. But even more importantly, these parents left with a renewed respect for the teacher. The teacher left with a renewed respect for parents and for the process of conflict itself. This situation resulted in creative growth through conflict.

Acknowledge Conflict among Staff

Another source of creative challenge occurs when there is conflict between staff members. Principals should never ignore this type of conflict because if it goes unchecked, it invariably leads to greater conflict, such as faculty taking sides. All too quickly faculty that felt a strong sense of community at the beginning of the year can become an armed camp. Principals can facilitate these kinds of conflict into communication opportunities by reminding teachers that it is healthy to disagree, then offering to provide a forum for discussion—not debate, discussion. By openly discussing the problem in a nonthreatening manner, faculty have an opportunity to give the issue serious thought, as well as an opportunity to give their input. Principals who model the challenge to view conflict as an opportunity for creativity say to their faculty by their actions: we do not all agree, but we can use our disagreement to become a better school and to become better people.

Tactical Actions
that Challenge the Imagination

Challenging the imagination through change and solving problems and conflicts in a way that encourages thinking creatively is a risky business. It can cause principals to feel that they are swimming upstream, battling the current. But even if this is so, it is also true, as Albert Einstein said, that sometimes "imagination is more important than knowledge" (in Glanz, 2002, p. 138). Thinking creatively is a challenge, but it has the potential to result in vibrant energy that builds leadership capacity and community throughout the school.

What actions can BRAVO principals implement to build relationships that value others while challenging the imagination to think creatively?

- Create a risk-free environment by not playing the "blame game."
- Be open to new ways of doing things.
- Never seek change just for the sake of change.
- Acknowledge every attempt at thinking outside the box.
- Encourage dialogue by providing time for idea exchanges.
- Consider problems from many perspectives.
- Critique, not criticize, when new ideas are tried and fail.
- Ask "what if?"
- Ask "why not?"
- Ask "why is that?"
- Act in terms of *how* and *when* a problem will be solved, not *if*.
- Do not let conflict become personal.
- Say little and listen more.

- Handle potential problems before they become conflicts.
- Be courteous and diplomatic.
- Deal with conflict immediately.

Remember, BRAVO principals build relationships with actions that value others through Challenging the Imagination.

Actions that Challenge the Imagination

Bring about Change
- Acknowledge that Change Is about People
- Involve Stakeholders

Solve Problems
- Use Creative Problem Solving
- Navigate Barriers

Manage Conflict
- Listen and Say Little
- Address Problems before They Become Conflicts
- Mediate Conflict between Parent and Teacher
- Acknowledge Conflict among Staff

5

Actions that Uphold High Standards: Dream Big

"No dream is too big for those with their eyes in the sky."

Buzz Aldrin
(in Glanz, 2002, p. 122)

Much controversy in our public schools today centers around one word: standards. Some think the standards are too low, some view the standards as too high, some say standards actually "dumb down" education, some say that the standards movement has led to a "test-crazy" environment, and on and on. Standards, however, are only a place to begin for a principal who builds relationships through valuing others, which reminds me of a story I once heard.

In the days before television there was a very famous radio commentator. His radio show received so much mail from listeners that he had six secretaries. One day, the show received a letter written on old, ragged paper. The letter, printed in pencil, said: "I am a shepherd in the North Dakota hills. I live alone, except for my dog who is my best friend. My fiddle is out of tune. Would you play an 'A' for me so that I can tune my fiddle?" The secretaries read the letter and laughed. Certainly the commentator would not be willing to take precious air time to respond to this request. Nevertheless, one day in the middle of his broadcast the newsman said, "Shepherd of the North Dakota hills, Shepherd of the North Dakota hills, this is your 'A,' this is your 'A.'" Then he played a strong, clear 'A.'

Without standards, principals would be like that shepherd in the hills, and their challenge to help students and faculty achieve would often be without direction. Too often today, educators and others interpret the standards movement in terms of test scores only, but upholding a standard is far more complex than evaluating an entire education system on the basis of a standardized test. Certainly, benchmark standards are an important foundational support that can ultimately lead to great dreams being achieved. It is the principal's job to foster and nourish an environment that upholds a *high* standard for all students, as well as for staff members. Look at it this way: The "A" allowed the musician to tune his instrument properly, a standard that is necessary. However, if the musician *only* played an "A" his beautiful music would have become only a noise.

Uphold High Standards
Through Acknowledging Responsibility

As educators, we understand the role principals play in setting the climate of the school. But principals today often are held to a standard of accountability that starts and ends with test preparation. I know of many principals who are told without hesitation, "either bring up the test scores or in two years you can look for a new job." (Sometimes, the superintendent is generous, and you have three years!) After all, according to the media in many states, the test scores say it all. Of course, we know that is not true. However, the test scores do provide an easily measurable standard that is (here we go again) a good place to begin, but not the place to end. This is why it is important for principals to acknowledge their responsibility to see that mandated minimum standards do not replace the need for high standards for everyone on the school campus.

Support for Every Child

A university teacher friend, who happens to be black, shared this story. She received much of her education in all-black schools. In the early 1960s when integration finally reached her community, her school was closed and all of the students were bused to the previously all-white school. She was an excellent student, at the top of her class. At her new school, she continued to excel. As she entered her senior year, she tried to make an appointment with the college counselor, but the meeting was delayed and delayed. Finally, she approached the counselor without an appointment and told him that she needed information about college scholarships. He responded that he understood her desire to go to college and maybe that would be possible, but, perhaps, she should consider other possibilities, just in case. Sadly, at her school there had been no one who acknowledged the responsibility to uphold a high standard for her and others like her.

That was over 30 years ago, but even though today's educators are becoming more and more aware that everyone must be held to a high standard, there are still schools where all children are not held accountable to that standard. Just a few weeks ago, one of my students in a principal certification class told about a teacher at her low-income school who prefaced many of her comments with, "These poor children, I can't change their home lives, how can I expect them to learn at school?" Finally, the principal called the teacher into his office and explained to her that it was true, she could not change the home lives of her children, but she could change their school life by expecting them to achieve certain standards. And he expected her to do just that! The principal fulfilled his responsibility to remind her of her obligation to support every child in reaching academic standards.

Verbalize Often

A principal is the voice of the school. Recently while on an airplane, I was grading a student's paper entitled, "Poverty and Achievement." I could see the young man sitting next to me craning his neck to read the paper. Finally, he spoke. "You must be a teacher." I explained that I taught classes in principalship. "So," he said, "Just what are you teaching your students?" Then he told me that he had grown up in an urban city, the youngest of eight children. His father left home when he was young, and his mother worked several jobs to support the children, all of whom eventually went to college and earned degrees. He then said, "The principal at my high school used to get on the loud speaker and say, 'It's my responsibility to see that every one at this school learns! We are here to learn and we are here to work. So, get busy! And have a good day!'" The young man then smiled at me and said, "Teach your students that!" Then he returned to his crossword puzzle.

A superintendent friend of mine tells about an incident that happened when he was working on his Master's degree and principal certificate. In mid-year, he was assigned as assistant principal at his school. Between his new school responsibilities, his family, and his school work there just was not time to complete everything as well as he would have liked. His final class assignment was due and he completed it rather hurriedly and turned it in, deciding that he could live with a B. Later that week he received a visit from his professor. She handed him the assignment—ungraded. When he asked her why she had not graded it, she replied, "I know how busy you are with your new assignment. But, this paper is just not up to the standard that I expect from you. In fact, I do not think it is up to the standard that you expect from yourself. I would rather have you turn this paper in a few days late than accept this lower standard. I am willing to wait… but just one week." As he tells this story, he emphasizes how important it was for him to have a high standard for himself, but, even more important, he says, was the support from his teacher whose words and actions not only demonstrated upholding a high standard for everyone, but held him accountable for that same high standard. This happened over ten years ago, and, now, in May, 2004, this superintendent will earn his doctorate in education… because a leader kept verbalizing the importance of high standards.

Uphold High Standards
Through Assessing Wisely

University professor Thomas Sergiovanni lamented that "If [your] job is on the line because of test scores, then you don't care about constructivism—you work to get the test scores up" (Allen, 2003, p. 1). Working to get the test scores up is necessary; and even though it frustrates many educators, it is a valid, important component of establishing a positive school culture, especially considering the number of schools and children who have slipped through the cracks over the years.

Understand that Standards Are Incremental

Faculty members are at different stages of growth; some are master teachers, some are beginning teachers, and some are in between. Our students are at different stages of growth; some are doing their very best, some are just getting by, and the rest fall somewhere between those extremes. This is why it is important to consider standards incrementally. In other words, principals should consider standards in three stages: good, better, best. Obviously, one cannot get to *best* without first achieving *good*. When my daughter was in nursery school she used to dance around the house singing a song that had a line in it that went something like this: "I'm a great big bundle of possibilities." That's what high standards should represent—good possibilities, better possibilities, and then the best possibilities.

Of course, this makes the job of the principal even more complicated, because principals need to recognize *levels* of standards. It is important to reach a minimum or good standard, but learning should not stop there. Once a minimum standard is reached, it is important to go one step further to get better. Once a *better* standard is achieved, it is important to be motivated to achieve the *best*. Are we content to be *good* principals? Do we want to be *better*? Do we want to be the *best* principal? Of course we do! As principals it is our job to motivate our faculty and our students to continue pursuing the possibilities inherent in their dreams of achievement. So, how do we know when a faculty member or a student is ready to be challenged and motivated to the next level of standard? Generally, it is through building supportive relationships that value others that we can begin to assess an individual's readiness for a higher standard.

Assess Teachers' Standards Intentionally

Miss Donald was in her fourth year of teaching. She had graduated from an alternative teaching certification program and had never done student teaching. When she interviewed, the hiring committee felt she had the potential to become a very good teacher. When she began teaching, she had little knowledge of what it was like to be in a real classroom. However, she was energetic, creative, intelligent, and willing to learn. She survived her first year of teaching. She survived the next year. One day, toward the end of her third year, the lead teacher commented to the principal that, "As a teacher, Miss Donald is pretty good." The principal thought back to that initial interview when they had expected she would be a much better teacher than *pretty good*.

Miss Donald was meeting a standard that was appropriate, but she was not meeting her potential. Together, the principal, lead teacher, and Miss Donald created a specific growth plan to help her move to the next standard. They spent time with her, which emphasized her own self-worth as a part of the faculty. They agreed to a more frequent classroom visit schedule that was supportive, rather than supervisory. Before too long, the principal was seeing glimpses of better teaching and knew that they were on their way to helping her become the best teacher that she could be.

Assess Teachers' Standards Naturally

Sometimes, principals assess the level of standard for a teacher or student without even realizing they are doing so. In fact, for principals who are committed to building and valuing relationships on their campus this is a natural action. Principals call a student into the office who is misbehaving or not achieving academically, and almost without thinking say, "I believe in you, I know you can do this." Sometimes, this comment falls on deaf ears, but other times it takes root and grows, and those words become a silent motivating standard bearer for years to come. A colleague tells of opening a wedding invitation from a girl who had been a fifth grader early in his career as a principal. A handwritten note fell onto the table. It read:

> I can't thank you enough for the day you called me to your office because my work was just not up to

par. We talked for a few minutes and then you told me that you expected more from me. From that moment on, I began to believe in myself in a way that I never had.

The principal remembered the student very well, but did not remember ever calling her into his office and certainly did not remember the conversation on that day. Yet, nearly 20 years had passed and that small action was still remembered. When my friend shared this with me, he pointed out that the note made him feel very good, for about ten minutes. Then, he began to think of all the opportunities he had missed, the times that he had failed to call a teacher or a child into his office and encourage them to reach for a higher standard. A principal's job is so demanding, it is easy to become satisfied with a minimal or good standard and stop there.

Uphold High Standards Through Challenging the Status Quo

A few weeks ago I was in Portland, Oregon, for a conference. I had never been there before, so a friend and I took a guided tour of the Portland area. The scenery was wild and beautiful. The white caps shimmered on the Columbia River and it snowed as we went to the top of Mt. Hood. As we drove down the highway, our guide pointed out that we were following the Oregon Trail—the same trail that Lewis and Clark had followed 150 years before. We visited Multnomah Falls and heard about the Indian pictographs that were on nearby cliffs. We stopped at the remodeled toll road where early pioneers had to either pay $2.00 to continue on the road or turn back.

As we experienced the rugged terrain, we reflected on what it could have been that made these pioneers leave their comfortable homes and forge ahead through difficulty and discomfort. What inner drive was the catalyst for these actions? Why were they not content with what they had or already knew? Surely, some inner, higher standard must have fueled their quest for something better, something beyond what they had already attained. It was upholding this standard that encouraged many early pioneers to go as far as their dreams would take them.

As school leaders we must challenge the status quo and uphold high standards that have the capacity to become even higher. By doing so, we can move beyond mandated account-ability systems based solely on standardized testing and, in-stead, lead our schools to something more meaningful. It is our job to motivate staff and students to consider new possi-bilities. We may have to move a teacher from her classroom to a different grade level. Or we may have a team that has worked together for so long they suffer from deadly "group think." Or perhaps we are too satisfied with being a Recog-nized campus, because Exemplary seems too hard to achieve. Just the other day, I heard an administrator say, "It's not my job to fire … it's my job to fire up!" Sometimes as principals we have to rock the boat a bit.

Nurture Dialogue

So, the question is how do we get faculty and students to move from comfort to a supposed higher standard that invari-ably results in some discomfort before the desired result is achieved? One way to do this is to nurture dialogue within the school. Involve teachers, students, and parents and talk about what is happening at the school, or what is not happening.

A junior high principal took over a school that had a Low Performing rating based on its test scores. He announced to faculty, students, and parents that he welcomed their input. They could come in at any time and tell him what they were experiencing at school and he would listen. Their desired so-lution might not ever happen, but he promised that when they left his office they would both have a different perspective of the situation. He conducted e-mail surveys several times dur-ing the year to gather input. PTA attendance that had previ-ously been minimal began to grow. He held very few manda-tory faculty meetings during the year, but he did hold volun-teer monthly "idea shares" for faculty, students, and parents. It took two years for the school to move from the state rating of Low Performing to an Acceptable rating based on their test scores. The school is now aiming for Recognized status and, when that is achieved, they will certainly aim for Exemplary status. As the principal fostered and nurtured dialogue, a school climate began to grow that was inviting; the status quo was no longer comfortable. At first, school personnel and students just wanted to pass the test to achieve a higher rating. But when this happened, they began to dream bigger than ever before.

Know about Your Faculty

Another way to challenge faculty to achieve higher standards is to know more about them. Ann Brown had taught seventh grade for 20 years. She was a master teacher who could do anything and do it well; in fact, she could do it better than anyone else in her school. But she was not a team player. After all, it was easier to do things herself. When she was in charge of a school program, she planned it all, and it was perfect. Her bulletin boards were a work of art. When there were students no one else could work with, they were placed in Ann's class; she could handle them. She was respected as a teacher, but her coworkers found her obnoxious and did not like her. She held herself to a very high standard as a teacher, but she had very low expectations for herself regarding interpersonal skills. In fact, they just did not exist.

A new principal was assigned to the school. Before too long, the principal began to notice Ann. She made several efforts to get to know this talented teacher with the "losing" personality better. Ann's story was interesting. She had put herself through college and graduated at the top of her class, but no one from her family had come to see her graduate. After teaching for about five years, she had begun to think about becoming a principal. But she was a single mother with no one to watch her son at night, and she could not afford college tuition on top of the college loans she was already paying. So Ann had thrown all of her energies into teaching seventh grade. After awhile, the desire to get her master's degree subsided, she liked being a teacher, she did not need friends, her son grew up, and she settled into a comfortable standard.

The new principal encouraged Ann to consider going back to school. Eventually, Ann enrolled in a principal program. She became energized and excited about her studies, occasionally sharing articles she was reading with other faculty. She began making connections with faculty that she had never made before. Her dreams were getting bigger.

Tactical Actions that Uphold High Standards

Principals who build relationships with actions that value others must uphold high standards for everyone on the campus. BRAVO principals acknowledge their responsibility for upholding high standards and recognize that standards are incremental and that they differ at different times for different individuals and under different circumstances. They also understand that high standards must be assessed wisely while at the same time challenging the status quo on campus.

What actions do principals who build relationships that value others model to uphold high standards?

- ♦ Acknowledge that they are responsible for what occurs on their campuses.
- ♦ Care that all students and faculty are held accountable to achieve.
- ♦ Recognize that standards can be minimum to maximum.
- ♦ Encourage others to achieve.
- ♦ Reflect on where people are in their growth.
- ♦ Implement growth plans that are specific.
- ♦ Involve teachers in creating their own growth plan.
- ♦ Understand that people need to be encouraged in different ways.
- ♦ Spend time with students and faculty.
- ♦ Talk with faculty and students about their dreams.
- ♦ Verbalize the need to move to higher standards.

- Remind teachers of why they became teachers in the first place.
- Share literature of successful reform efforts.
- Talk openly about what they have learned through failure.
- Model life-long learning.

Dreaming big is necessary to achieving beyond ourselves. The writer Zora Neale Hurston said that her mother "exhorted her children at every opportunity to 'jump at de sun.' We might not land on the sun, but, at least, we would get off the ground" (in Eisen, 1995, p. 167). When principals uphold high standards they encourage students and teachers to dream bigger than they might otherwise have done. Dreaming big is the only way we will ever get off the ground to even get close to reaching the sky.

Remember, BRAVO principals build relationships with actions that value others through Upholding High Standards.

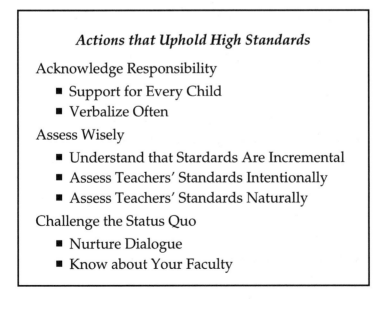

Actions that Uphold High Standards

Acknowledge Responsibility
- Support for Every Child
- Verbalize Often

Assess Wisely
- Understand that Stardards Are Incremental
- Assess Teachers' Standards Intentionally
- Assess Teachers' Standards Naturally

Challenge the Status Quo
- Nurture Dialogue
- Know about Your Faculty

6

Actions that Are Courageous: Master Fear

"Courage is resistance to fear, mastery of fear—not absence of fear."

Mark Twain
(The Columbia World
of Quotations, 1996)

In 1846, five-year-old Sarah Roberts was beginning school. Because she was black, Sarah would have to walk past five schools to reach her all-black school. Feeling that this was not right, her father, Benjamin, took her to the first school and tried to enroll her. She was denied. He then took her to each of the other four schools. But at each school, she was denied admission. Sarah's father sued the City of Boston. In 1849, her case reached the Massachusetts State Supreme Court where her lawyer, the abolitionist Charles Sumner, argued:

> The school is the little world in which the child is trained for the larger world of life, beginning there those relations of Equality which the constitution and the laws promise to all. I conclude that there is but one kind of public school, free to all … excluding none, comprehending all. (Mondale & Patton, 2001, p. 44)

Chief Justice Lemuel Shaw ruled against Sarah Roberts.

Yet, this singular act of courage in 1846 of a black father and his five-year-old daughter served as an act of hope to another father over 100 years later when Reverend Oliver Brown walked his eight-year-old daughter, Linda, into the office of a Topeka, Kansas, school principal. She, too, was turned away. But this time, in 1954, the U.S. Supreme Court remembered Sarah Roberts and cited her attorney, Charles Sumner, in *Brown v. Board of Education of Topeka*. The Court announced that " … [the opportunity of an education] … is a right which must be made available to all on equal terms …" (Mondale & Patton, 2001, p. 138).

Throughout the school day principals are faced with issues that require courage. We mediate, sometimes on a minute-by-minute basis, problems among personnel, students, parents, and other community stakeholders. We make statements to the media and must weigh every word. We constantly must concern ourselves with saying and doing just the right thing in just the right way to avoid litigation. As principals, we must know what we believe, we must advocate for others, we must be willing to stay the course to build relationships with actions that value others. Acts of courage brought about the beginning of the end of legally segregated schools in American public schools. Perhaps our acts of courage seem small in the face of this, but I doubt that when Benjamin and Sarah Roberts took the first fearful steps of their momentous walk that they ever dreamed it would ultimately change public schools forever.

Courageous Actions by Knowing What You Believe

Educators constantly talk about the importance of the school belief, vision, philosophy, or mission statement; and, as a result, today most schools have these "guiding truths" posted in classrooms, hallways, and policy manuals. But a school belief statement is absolutely meaningless unless it is a living document that is modeled, first of all, in the actions of the principal. It is often when we base our actions on those very idealistic belief statements that we most need to draw on our courage. In fact, Jeffrey Glanz (2002) writes, "without courage, educational leaders become mere technicians, administrative guardians, and nothing more than custodians of the institution" (p. 90). Therefore, a foundational component of being able to act courageously on what we believe is to know what we believe.

A few years ago, Bob, a colleague of mine, was a first-year principal who had just moved to a rural city in the Deep South. He hired a female teacher for upper level mathematics classes in the high school who was both qualified and experienced. This had been a particularly difficult position to fill with very few applicants—salaries in that area were at minimum state levels, and calculus teachers were never easy to find. The newly hired teacher was a single mother with three children. Once the school year began, Bob was delighted to find that she was an excellent teacher. However, he soon became aware that the other teachers made no effort to get to know her. She seemed to have no friends. He even noticed that her three biracial children were not accepted into the school community. She drove a beat-up old car to school and rented a fairly run-down house on the edge of town. Clearly, she was struggling financially.

Then one day, the teacher's youngest child, who was a diabetic, collapsed at school. Bob followed the ambulance in his car to the hospital where he stayed until the doctor came and assured her that her son was going to be fine. Before leaving to go back to school, he called his secretary who told him that the other two children were waiting in the office and she asked him what she should do.

As Bob drove the 30 miles to the school to pick up the two little boys, he reflected on his beliefs. Why had he become an educator in the first place? He remembered his early idealism and how eager he had been to help children. When he had completed his master's degree in the principalship, he could not wait to get his first assignment. He had started this year looking forward to working with the teachers and hoping to bring all of them together as a team, uniting under a vision of being the "best place for students to learn." He knew what he believed, but had he been acting on that belief? What was he doing to lead others to act on that belief?

Confront Your Own Weakness

Bob was shocked and disappointed at his own lack of action. He had allowed the faculty at the school to ostracize this teacher; he saw it happening and he had done nothing. He had allowed her children to be ignored by the other students. By saying nothing, he had allowed this to happen. He tried to justify his actions. After all, it was his first year as principal, as well as his first year in the community. He knew that, politically, it was important for him to establish himself in the community before he could bring about changes in some of the long-held beliefs. Regardless, he admitted to himself that he was simply afraid to confront this situation.

Apologize

At the end of the next school day, Bob called a meeting. His hands were sweating, and he could hardly breathe. He stood at the front of the room and told the teachers that he had made a bad decision. He had seen what was happening to the teacher and to her children, and he had chosen to be silent. He reminded them of the school's vision statement and of his own reason for becoming an educator. Then he said, "This will not continue ... how can we work together to change this?" Change was slow, but by the end of the year, the math teacher had become an integral part of the faculty, the children were being accepted, and the community seemed a shade more welcoming.

John Blanchard and Margaret McBride in their book *The One Minute Apology* say that when we realize that we have made a mistake we must surrender and take full responsibility for our actions. Then we must act as soon as possible to acknowledge what we did wrong. To apologize with integrity we complete our apology with forgiving ourselves, making amends, and committing to changing our behavior. Apologizing to the people we work with, students, or parents is not an easy thing to do. In fact, just thinking about it can cause our blood pressure to rise. It takes courage to acknowledge our errors. John Wayne was right when he said, "Courage is being scared to death—but saddling up anyway" (Quotationspage.com). Having the courage to admit error, apologize, and then "saddle up" or work together to correct it is often the very catalyst needed by others to acknowledge their vulnerability and activate their own courage. After all, courage is contagious.

Courageous Actions by Advocating for Others

As educators build relationships that value others, we must remember that our first priority is always the students. That means that circumstances must consistently be viewed under the umbrella of "what is best for students." Sometimes advocating for students not only takes courage, but also requires tremendous energy, as we consider the battles needed to be fought to do what we consider is best for them. This is why it is so crucial to continually revitalize our vision for becoming educators.

Mohammed is a devout Muslim teenager from North Africa. He has only been in a U.S. school for three months and cannot speak, write, or read English. He dreams of going back to North Africa to live with his grandfather who taught him about farming and the oral history of his land. Mohammed is in an ESL geometry class, but he is failing. His teacher insists that he cannot learn. Who will advocate for Mohammed?

Angelina is from Brazil. She speaks English and Spanish but has difficulty expressing complex thoughts in English. She failed the nine-week algebra test. When the teacher told her that she would be calling her parents to notify them, Angelina pleaded with her not to call. She lives with an uncle "who places his hands on me where they should not be" and an aunt who does not like her. She is afraid they will send her back to Brazil. Who will advocate for Angelina?

Who will advocate for Mohammed, Angelina, and the countless other students who come through the doors of our schools? Who will advocate for the children who are abused, poor, and under served who sit in our classrooms? Who will advocate for the children who rarely see a parent and are angry and alone? Who will advocate for the children who struggle academically? Who will advocate for the children identified in our schools as gifted and talented? Who will advocate for the children in our schools who are bullied and mistreated by others? Who will advocate? If not the principal, then who? It will take courage, but, if the principal does not give voice to their silent cries, many of our children will never reach their potential.

Recognize that Risk Exists

Principals are faced with hard decisions and must recognize that risk exists when making hard decisions. As with all risks, we win some and lose some. But principals who build relationships with actions that value others consider the risks and look for win-win situations. Over the years, I have known principals who had to reassign close friends, replace well-loved coaches, fire a best friend's son or daughter, suspend or expel children of board members, and the list goes on, all actions in the interest of "what is best for students." In all of these situations, relationships were altered, for sure. But when principals openly commit to advocating for others in a way that is consistent with the values and beliefs of the school, after the hurt of their actions subsides, feelings of respect and sometimes even admiration often return. But sometimes, they do not.

Last year, an award-winning, 30-year veteran first grade teacher had a stroke. Three months after her stroke, she was much improved, but her speech was still seriously impaired, as was her mobility. One day her daughter came to the principal and suggested that it was time for her mother to come back to her first grade class. She was feeling much better and even her doctor had agreed that she could resume some work. After all, her daughter said, "It would be the best thing in the world for Mother to be back with her students—she loves teaching." The principal pointed out the demands of a first grade class and suggested several alternate assignments she might do as she continued recuperating, but to no avail. The daughter insisted that her mother must come back to her beloved first graders. In fact, she had already discussed this with her husband (did I forget to mention that he was the president of the school board?) who had suggested that an aide could be hired to help out in the classroom (even though there was no money for other extras in the district).

The school district was a close-knit community. The principal knew that to deny this request could have very serious repercussions. But he also knew that this was not the best decision for the students in the classroom at this time. It took courage, but when he reflected upon his responsibility to advocate for student learning, he knew there was only one decision to make. Knowing what he believed and understanding his commitment to be an advocate for students made it easier to have the courage to say "no."

Realize that Decisions
Rarely Please Everyone

Generally, no matter how hard we try our decisions will not make everyone happy. Knowing that our absolute best effort has been given to create a solution that could be agreeable to both parties makes it easier to live with decisions that do not please everyone. Having a framework of guiding questions to follow can help with these hard-to-make decisions. I have found these five questions to be helpful in clarifying problems and identifying possible solutions:

1. What is the absolute best decision for both sides?
2. What would be the short-term effects of those "best decisions"?
3. How would I respond if I only knew the problem, and not the people?
4. What decision is consistent with what I believe?
5. What will be the long-term effects of my decision?

By going through this process, principals are able to define each issue with greater clarity, which strengthens their courage to make difficult decisions.

Courageous Actions
by Staying the Course

Courage over the long term is not easy to sustain. But to maintain trusting staff, student, and parent relationships, principals must continuously commit to act with courage toward *everyone* on campus. We all know principals who have the courage of a general when it comes to supporting some of the faculty, or certain students, but not when it comes to supporting others. This arbitrary courage is confusing and creates poor relationships among the entire staff.

Unfortunately, making one courageous decision doesn't make us paragons of courage. Each circumstance that arises and presents a challenge causes us to agonize all over again. However, it is not always being afraid of the outcome that causes our anxiety, sometimes we just are not sure which is the best decision to make. When this happens, to act at all is often an act of courage. Eleanor Roosevelt exhorted people to "gain strength, courage and confidence by every experience in which you really stop to look fear in the face. ... You must do the thing you think you cannot do ..." (Quotations.page.com). As leaders act courageously and survive to tell about it, we gain confidence to act more courageously when the next dilemma occurs.

Recently a student picked up a note that had fallen onto the floor of a high school hallway. She opened the note and saw a heading "Kill" and then a list of names. On the list were several teacher names, the principal's name, student athletes, and cheerleaders. At first the student thought it was just a silly note... but then, she decided that she should at least take it to the principal's office. The principal read the note and immediately began to feel sick to his stomach. The note had a name on it, so he called the student into his office. This led to bringing in four other boys. A search of the boys' cars was conducted. Guns were found. Of course the police were called in and the boys arrested.

But the principal knew that this was just the beginning of a media frenzy for the school. Sure enough, throughout the state, the headlines screamed about the episode at school. What could the principal do to restore calm at the school? How could he assure parents and students that the school was a safe place? He went to the superintendent and together they decided that they would hold a town meeting. The meeting was scheduled to be held on a night when many of the area churches met. The churches shortened their meeting times to encourage people to attend the school meeting. The police chief was invited to speak, as was the district attorney. That night over 800 people crowded into the school's auditorium.

It took courage, but the principal had done more than put a stop to a violent action by following up on the note that had been found. Of course, he had seen to it that the offending boys were disciplined. But, more than that, he had brought the community together to understand that school violence was not just a school problem, but a problem that needed the response and support of the collective community. He had chosen to stay the course and see the problem through to a more complete resolution which took a courage that he admits he did not know he had.

Learn from Previous Experiences

Principals who reflect on previous experiences of their own as teachers and parents fuel their own courage to act. One of my aspiring principal students is Hispanic and her husband is East Indian. When her son was in the fifth grade, the other children began making fun of his father's ethnicity by saying his dad "was a yaki from paki." When this happened, her son realized that he actually looked more like his Hispanic mother and became embarrassed that his dad looked like the people some of the children in the class made fun of. Her son decided that he no longer wanted his dad to pick him up at school. They eventually overcame this painful situation by dealing with it as a family. When my student shared this she pointed out that as a principal she would be more sensitive and courageous in dealing with this type of issue because of her personal experience.

Drawing from our own experiences both personally and professionally can be a tremendous resource to increase our courage. Sharing these experiences is a catalyst to building relationships that reminds us of our own humanity and the connections that are built as we draw strength from one another's experiences. When a teacher is going through a really bad time in the classroom, it helps that the principal can remember a similar event and share what helped her get through it. Or when a parent is worried over a wayward child, a principal can share about children who struggled through adolescence and are now successful members of the community. When we read or hear about a problem at a neighboring school, BRAVO principals pick up the phone or e-mail that principal to share their own experience or just to voice their support. These seemingly small acts of sharing experiences provide strong connections demonstrating that a little courage can go a long way, and help us to keep our perspective. As a dear principal

friend of mine used to remind me when I found myself in
turmoil, "This too shall pass."

Maintain a Sense of Humor

Another tool that helps principals act courageously is an
active sense of humor. Even though laughing at ourselves can
sometimes make us seem more vulnerable, laughter is a wonderful way to build a sense of community within the school.
There is something about laughter that brings people together
even in difficult times. I have heard the saying, "nothing
builds friendships like sharing a common enemy." Sharing
laughter can also build strong relationships. In fact, laughter
paves the way for courage because it lightens the gloom of a
difficult, anxious situation.

I am reminded of a particularly difficult time at one of my
schools. When the leadership team walked into the conference
room for our weekly meeting, there was no friendly banter;
the room was quiet and our faces were somber. Then the middle school principal put a tape recorder on the table; she hit the
Play button, and the room filled with the sounds of Johnny
Paycheck singing "Take this Job and Shove It!" I still smile
thinking about it. I know the laughter we shared when listening to that song gave us more courage to make the very difficult decisions we were facing.

Tactical Actions
that Are Courageous.

Courageous actions can cause our hearts to race, our
palms to sweat, and our nights to be sleepless. In today's
world, there is likely not a principal among us who has not
gone to bed with visions of themselves hiding under a desk in
fear, and rightly so. We live in turbulent times. Someone once
said that "if God had wanted us to be courageous, he would
not have given us legs." There have been times when I certainly thought that the best solution would be *run*, and let
someone else make the hard decisions. BRAVO principals
master these fears when they know what they believe, advocate for others, and commit to staying the course.

What actions can BRAVO principals do to build relationships that value others while acting courageously?

- Reflect on personal and professional beliefs.
- Reevaluate beliefs.
- Speak openly about guiding beliefs.
- Model guiding beliefs.
- Provide time for faculty to participate in reflection and reevaluation of beliefs.
- Confront weaknesses openly.
- Accept the responsibility of a wrong decision or no decision.
- Apologize when an error is made.
- Commit to not making the error again.
- Learn from mistakes.
- Ask for help.
- Remember, "we" is always better than "me."
- Advocate for student learning.
- Identify risks.
- Make every effort to achieve win-win decisions for everyone.
- Be patient while people work through personal and professional hurts from decisions that have been made.
- Recognize that everyone will not agree with your decisions.
- Create a guiding framework around what you believe to support decision making.
- Learn from earlier experiences.
- Share laughter.

Remember, BRAVO principals build relationships with actions that value others through being Courageous

Courageous Actions

Know What You Believe

- Confront Your Own Weakness
- Apologize

Advocate for Others

- Recognize that Risk Exists
- Realize that Decisions Rarely Please Everyone

Stay the Course

- Learn from Previous Experiences
- Maintain a Sense of Humor

7

Conclusion

"It is not so much where we stand, as in the direction we are moving. To reach the port of heaven, we must sail sometimes with the wind and sometimes against it—but we must sail, and not drift, nor lie at anchor."

(Author Unknown)

Recently, a friend invited me to a gathering at her house. When I arrived, I noticed that most of the people who were there fit into one of two categories: they were either teachers who had worked together or they were our former students. As I went from group to group visiting, one phrase reverberated, "Remember when you (we) did … ?" Throughout the evening, we talked about things we had done in relation to one another. Even though some of these associations occurred over 20 years ago, we were still talking about actions that had happened at school back then and the relationships that had resulted.

A superintendent friend of mine contends that we should define people by *who* they are, not by *what* they do. After all, he argues, we are "not human doings, but human beings." And though there are certainly occasions to define people by who they are, people are most likely to be known by their actions, or their lack of actions. In other words, it is nearly impossible to separate the essence of who we are from our actions. The truth is, who we are is based on how we act—or is it, how we act is based on who we are? Which comes first, the chicken or the egg? This is not the forum for debate, but it illustrates how inextricably related are our actions and our very being; in fact, our actions do speak louder than our words. The same is true for leaders.

Leaders live daily with dilemmas and problems that challenge the structure, policy, and practice of the school, and at the same time they are charged with meeting the needs of people. Meeting the needs of people can only occur when we connect with people, and we can only connect with people when we build relationships that are grounded in valuing others.

Within the leadership literature there is no one accepted definition that defines the actions of leadership. Instead, leadership is viewed in a variety of ways that all can influence the actions of a leader. Some believe that leadership is primarily good management. Others would say that leaders are born, not made. Still others would say that leaders either have or they don't have this elusive quality called leadership. Others might define leadership within the context of those who follow, or relate it to the position someone holds. Some identify leadership by the effect it has on others, or its ability to bring about change. I would not even begin to define leadership. Yet, I do argue that leadership that is committed to building relationships with actions that value others has the opportunity to change the world.

The phrases "No Child Left Behind," "Success for All," "Every Child Can Learn," and many more just like these are indelibly etched on the walls of schools and in the hearts and minds of today's educators. But they are just words. Without appropriate actions by school leaders, teachers will not be free to teach and some children will not learn. Leadership that emphasizes relationships allows principals to see "more in teachers than teachers sometimes see in themselves—just as good teachers see more in students than students know they have" (Palmer, 1998, p.159). Max DePree (1989) calls this relationship "covenantal" because it fills needs, personally and professionally, and "enables work to have meaning and to be fulfilling" (p. 60).

There are times when we will not know where our actions will end. When Charles Sumner argued in 1849 that Sarah Roberts be allowed to attend a school near her home, he lost. Over 100 years later, his argument acted as a catalyst for the U.S. Supreme Court when it acted to right this wrong. Our victories may not seem so grand. We share our power with a school committee. We encourage a teacher to consider going back to work on a master's degree. We support a teacher who is having difficulty. We reprimand students and point out that they have unmet leadership potential. We help an out-of-work husband find a job. We locate a babysitter for a teacher. We create a flexible schedule for our students. We treat a parent who speaks no English with respect. We place a handicapped child in a regular classroom. We intervene for a student who is being bullied. We challenge faculty to creatively find resources. We advocate for a higher academic standard. We stand up for what we believe is right. We courageously stay the course in the face of conflict. We assume our action ends with the deed. Yet, an Indian father helped a child imprint his small hand on the wall of a cliff in Arizona. Three thousand years later, this act called out to me and reminded me of the importance of our actions. The deed had been done long ago, but the action itself had transcended time.

BRAVO principals build relationships that value others when their actions empower others, support the work of learning and teaching, are respectful of all, challenge imaginations, uphold high standards, and are courageous. Through conscious, intentional acts of valuing others, school leaders leave a timeless, indelible impression on the hearts and minds of those with whom they come in contact. Through this legacy of leadership, schools can become places that value others. As principals lead by building relationships with actions that value others, slowly, one teacher at a time, one student at a time, one family at a time, we can see the world change. Bravo principal!

Building Relationships
with Actions that Value Others

Empowering Actions
- Create a Shared Vision
- Establish Trust
- Build Leadership at Every Level

Supportive Actions
- Communicate Effectively
- Offer Encouragement
- Recognize Needs
- Provide Resources

Respectful Actions
- Are Fair
- Care
- Celebrate Diversity

Actions that Challenge the Imagination
- Bring about Change
- Solve Problems
- Manage Conflict

Actions that Uphold High Standards
- Acknowledge Responsibility
- Assess Wisely
- Challenge the Status Quo

Courageous Actions
- Know What You Believe
- Advocate for Others
- Stay the Course

References

Allen, R. (2003). Building school culture in an age of accountability: Principals lead through sharing tasks. *Education Update, 45*(7), 1, 3, 7–8.

Blanchard, K., & McBride, M. (2003). *The one minute apology.* New York: William Morrow.

Burns, J. (1978). *Leadership.* New York: Harper Collins.

Csikszentmihalyi, M. (1990). *Flow: The psychology of optimal experience.* New York: HarperCollins.

Dare to succeed: A treasury of inspiration and wisdom for life and career. (1991). Tulsa, OK: Honor Books.

DePree, M. (1989). *Leadership is an art.* New York: Bantam Doubleday Books.

Eisen, A. (1995). *A woman's journey: Reflections on life, love, and happiness.* Kansas City, MO: Ariel Books.

Glanz, J. (2002). *Finding your leadership style.* Alexandria, VA: ASCD.

Hare, D., & Heap, J. L. (2001a). *Teacher recruitment and retention strategies in the Midwest: Where are they and do they work?* Naperville, IL: North Central Regional Educational Laboratory.

Hare, D., & Heap, J. L. (2001b). *Effective teacher recruitment and retention strategies in the Midwest: Who is making use of them?* Naperville, IL: North Central Regional Educational Laboratory.

Hargreaves, A. (1994). *Changing teachers, changing times.* New York: Teachers College Press.

Harris, S. (2000). Behave yourself. Good principals believe that leadership is at all levels of the school. *Principal Leadership, 1* (3), 36–39.

Harris, S., & Lowery, S. (2003). *Standards-based leadership: A case study book for the principalship.* Lanham, MD: ScarecrowEducation.

Hord, S., Rutherford, W., Huling-Austin, L., & Hall, G. (1987). *Taking charge of change.* Alexandria, VA: Association for Supervision and Curriculum Development.

Kouzes, J., & Posner, B. (1995). *The leadership challenge: How to keep getting extraordinary things done in organizations.* San Francisco: Jossey-Bass.

Kouzes, J., & Posner, B. (2002). *The leadership challenge (3rd ed.).* San Francisco: Jossey-Bass.

Lambert, L. (2003). *Leadership for capacity for lasting school improvement.* Alexandria, VA: ASCD.

Melley, C. (2001). ET's Robinson: Address diversity in tomorrow's workforce today. *Education Testing Service.* Retrieved on October 17, 2003, from http://www.ets.org/search 97cgi/s97_cgi

Mondale, S., & Patton, S. (Eds.). (2001). *School: The story of American public education.* Boston: Beacon Press.

Palmer, P. J. (1998). *The courage to teach: Exploring the inner landscape of a teacher's life.* San Francisco: Jossey-Bass.

Peter, L. J. (1977). *Peter's quotations: Ideas for our time.* New York: William Morrow & Co., Inc.

Quotationspage.com. Retrieved December 21, 2003, from http://www.quotationspage.com/quotes/

Safire, W., & Safir, L. (1990). *Leadership: A treasury of great quotations for those who aspire to lead.* New York: Barnes & Noble.

Sergiovanni, T. (1992). *Moral leadership.* San Francisco: Jossey Bass.

The Columbia World of Quotations. (1996). Number 62113. Retrieved December 21, 2003, from http://www.bartleby.com/66/13/62113.html

Verdugo, R., & Schneider, J. (1999). Quality schools, safe schools: A theoretical and empirical discussion. *Education & Urban Society, 31*(3), 286–308.